COUNCIL *on*
FOREIGN
RELATIONS

Council Special Report No. 85
January 2020

Implementing Grand Strategy Toward China
Twenty-Two U.S. Policy Prescriptions

Robert D. Blackwill

The Council on Foreign Relations (CFR) is an independent, nonpartisan membership organization, think tank, and publisher dedicated to being a resource for its members, government officials, business executives, journalists, educators and students, civic and religious leaders, and other interested citizens in order to help them better understand the world and the foreign policy choices facing the United States and other countries. Founded in 1921, CFR carries out its mission by maintaining a diverse membership, with special programs to promote interest and develop expertise in the next generation of foreign policy leaders; convening meetings at its headquarters in New York and in Washington, DC, and other cities where senior government officials, members of Congress, global leaders, and prominent thinkers come together with Council members to discuss and debate major international issues; supporting a Studies Program that fosters independent research, enabling CFR scholars to produce articles, reports, and books and hold roundtables that analyze foreign policy issues and make concrete policy recommendations; publishing *Foreign Affairs*, the preeminent journal on international affairs and U.S. foreign policy; sponsoring Independent Task Forces that produce reports with both findings and policy prescriptions on the most important foreign policy topics; and providing up-to-date information and analysis about world events and American foreign policy on its website, CFR.org.

The Council on Foreign Relations takes no institutional positions on policy issues and has no affiliation with the U.S. government. All views expressed in its publications and on its website are the sole responsibility of the author or authors.

Council Special Reports (CSRs) are concise policy briefs, produced to provide a rapid response to a developing crisis or contribute to the public's understanding of current policy dilemmas. CSRs are written by individual authors—who may be CFR fellows or acknowledged experts from outside the institution—in consultation with an advisory committee, and are intended to take sixty days from inception to publication. The committee serves as a sounding board and provides feedback on a draft report. It usually meets twice—once before a draft is written and once again when there is a draft for review; however, advisory committee members, unlike Task Force members, are not asked to sign off on the report or to otherwise endorse it. Once published, CSRs are posted on CFR.org.

For further information about CFR or this Special Report, please write to the Council on Foreign Relations, 58 East 68th Street, New York, NY 10065, or call the Communications office at 212.434.9888. Visit our website, CFR.org.

Copyright © 2020 by the Council on Foreign Relations ®, Inc.

All rights reserved.

Printed in the United States of America.

This report may not be reproduced in whole or in part, in any form beyond the reproduction permitted by Sections 107 and 108 of the U.S. Copyright Law Act (17 U.S.C. Sections 107 and 108) and excerpts by reviewers for the public press, without express written permission from the Council on Foreign Relations.

To submit a letter in response to a Council Special Report for publication on our website, CFR.org, you may send an email to publications@cfr.org. Alternatively, letters may be mailed to us at: Publications Department, Council on Foreign Relations, 58 East 68th Street, New York, NY 10065. Letters should include the writer's name, postal address, and daytime phone number. Letters may be edited for length and clarity, and may be published online. Please do not send attachments. All letters become the property of the Council on Foreign Relations and will not be returned. We regret that, owing to the volume of correspondence, we cannot respond to every letter.

This report is printed on paper that is FSC ® Chain-of-Custody Certified by a printer who is certified by BM TRADA North America Inc.

CONTENTS

FOREWORD

American disillusionment with China and with the U.S.-China relationship has increased sharply in recent years. This thinking crosses party lines, fueled by China's internal and external policies alike. China's economic practices, including its theft and forced transfer of intellectual property and the lack of market access for U.S. firms, are especially unpopular. Adding to the shift in American attitudes is the view that China has become more assertive abroad (in pressing its claims to the South China Sea, its policy toward Taiwan, and its dealings with neighbors) and at home, where the Chinese government has begun a campaign of forced detentions in Xinjiang, is tightening its control over Hong Kong, and is constricting civil society throughout the country.

This is the context in which Robert D. Blackwill, the Henry A. Kissinger senior fellow for U.S. foreign policy here at the Council on Foreign Relations, presents this new Council Special Report. Blackwill and I both believe the modern U.S.-China relationship can usefully be divided into four phases. The first phase, which lasted from the establishment of the People's Republic of China until rapprochement under President Richard M. Nixon, was one of open hostility. The United States much preferred that the Communists not win the internal struggle for power that resumed following World War II, and after they did, the two countries fought on opposite sides during the Korean War. The second phase, animated by a shared antipathy toward the Soviet Union, lasted until the end of the Cold War; it was one in which the United States and China worked together to counter the Soviet threat. In the wake of the Soviet Union's collapse in 1991, the relationship entered its third phase, typified by increasing investment, trade, and China's integration into the global economy. Now, without a strategic rationale for the relationship and a questioning of the benefits of close economic ties, we are in a fourth phase that has yet to be defined but is increasingly characterized much more by competition than cooperation.

Blackwill argues the United States needs a new grand strategy to navigate this fourth phase of the Sino-American relationship. Akin to senior figures in the U.S. government who historically have decided China policy, Blackwill is not a country specialist but rather a foreign policy generalist who brings extensive senior-level government experience, along with a rigorous strategic mind, to bear on this critical issue. He contends that neither the United States nor China will be able to maintain or establish primacy in Asia. Instead, in order to uphold stability in the region, Blackwill writes, the United States will need to balance China's growing power while simultaneously maintaining the ability to work with the country to address common challenges, such as climate change and nuclear proliferation. This relationship will require that both countries do more to respect each other's vital national interests, a concept that he defines with precision. It will also place a premium on effective statecraft.

As the title promises, Blackwill presents no less than twenty-two policy prescriptions. All are predicated on his belief that "to preserve a crucial U.S. role in shaping the global system remains the central objective of U.S. grand strategy in the twenty-first century." His proposals begin domestically, with emphasis on reforms to better compete with China, such as modernizing America's infrastructure, improving its education system, and working creatively to harness next-generation technologies. He then lists changes the United States should make to its foreign policy, from spending fewer resources on the Middle East, to improving ties with allies in Asia and Europe, shifting military resources to Asia, and seeking a more constructive relationship with Russia.

I expect that many readers will disagree with some of Blackwill's analysis and proposed policies. That is not surprising given the breadth of what is covered. But total agreement is not necessary to derive real benefit from what is written here. Blackwill's thoroughly researched and tightly argued piece provides a foundation and a jumping-off point that will help observers and policymakers alike better understand the choices central to the modern U.S.-China relationship. There are few, if any, more important choices to be made in all of U.S. foreign policy, as no other bilateral relationship will do more to define the nature of this century.

Richard N. Haass
President
Council on Foreign Relations
December 2019

ACKNOWLEDGMENTS

This Council Special Report greatly benefited from the dozens of specific suggestions and valuable improvements by Henry Kissinger, Graham Allison, Kurt Campbell, Elizabeth C. Economy, Frank Gavin, Stephen Hadley, Amy Myers Jaffe, Shankar Menon, Mira Rapp-Hooper, Gary Roughead, Adam Segal, Philip Zelikow, and Robert Zoellick. To pay attention to smart people always makes one smarter, or as George Shultz once observed, "Listening is an underrated way of acquiring knowledge." I took most of their suggested fixes but, as they will see, not all. I am especially grateful to Dr. Kissinger for his friendship, inspiration, and guidance throughout virtually my entire adult life. I also thank Council on Foreign Relations (CFR) President Richard N. Haass for his review and comments. I appreciate the work of Patricia Dorff and the CFR Publications team for editorial contributions. My special thanks to Daniel Clay for his extensive research for this report.

The analysis and conclusions herein are my responsibility alone.

Robert D. Blackwill

To build peace on reciprocal restraint; to suffuse our concept of order with our country's commitment to freedom; to strive for peace without abdication and for order without unnecessary confrontation—therein resides the ultimate test of American statesmanship.

—Henry Kissinger, *Years of Upheaval*

Never before has a new world order had to be assembled from so many different perceptions, or on so global a scale. Nor has any previous order had to combine the attributes of the historic balance-of-power systems with global democratic opinion and the exploding technology of the contemporary period.

—Henry Kissinger, *World Order*

You never see the end of things when you're in them.

—Joseph Kanon, *Leaving Berlin: A Novel*

Forgetting our objectives is the most frequent of all acts of stupidity.

—Friedrich Nietzsche, *Human, All Too Human*

INTRODUCTION

Both the U.S. and Chinese governments currently strive for illusionary primacy in the Indo-Pacific.[1] Washington possessed primacy for five decades and in its bureaucratic bones and muscle memory still wants it, whatever it says publicly; and Beijing, mistakenly inspired by alleged long-term U.S. international decline, implements a grand strategy to acquire it.[2] However, China's primacy in Asia would be radically different than that exercised by the United States in the second half of the twentieth century. Nothing in its history suggests that China would provide global public goods, work for an open and egalitarian order, or set rules that it systematically followed. Rather, the primacy that China imposed historically was of a hierarchical order in which it sought respect, obedience, and anticipatory compliance.

Nevertheless, and as attractive as it may be in theory, Washington should accept that under foreseeable circumstances and given the many impressive dimensions of rising Chinese power, it no longer has the option of broadly based primacy in Asia.[3] At the same time, the United States certainly has the national and alliance resources, if adequately deployed, to prevent Chinese primacy in the Indo-Pacific.[4]

The key to reestablish Asian stability for the period ahead is for the United States, with its allies, partners, and friends, to successfully balance Chinese power, and at the same time to conduct artful diplomacy with Beijing.[5] But it is increasingly obvious that neither the United States nor China has developed concepts on how to act in regional and global systems in which no nation has primacy.[6] If both foolishly continue to actively seek primacy in the Indo-Pacific, few consequential compromises will be advanced or accepted by Washington or Beijing. With little or no willingness by either side to take the other's vital national interests into account, the road opens to sustained confrontation and perhaps even, in extremis, military conflict.[7]

However, such a dangerous outcome is far from inevitable. It can be avoided if the political leadership in both countries displays sustained caution in a conceptual framework with these objectives:

- reach a broad understanding over what constitutes their respective vital national interests (this is far more important than resolving current bilateral disagreements on trade);

- construct off-ramps through diplomacy to avert confrontations over mutually incompatible vital national interests;[8]

- avoid making subsidiary issues tests of national strength and prestige;

- compromise on less important matters;

- muzzle inflamed government public rhetoric regarding the policies and actions of the other;

- search for areas to cooperate intensively on global governance, such as climate change, the world economy, and nonproliferation;

- accept that for the foreseeable future the United States and China will have incompatible political systems and two fundamentally opposed concepts about the sources of political legitimacy and how best to organize societies; and

- reject regime change as a policy objective in word and deed.[9]

But even if all these goals are more or less realized, each nation is likely to regard the other as a strategic adversary. They have different histories, political cultures and values, perceived vital national interests, long-term foreign policy goals, and visions of domestic and world order. And with each seeking primary leadership in Asia, the United States and China are unlikely to reach a sustained and stable equilibrium in the region and globally anytime soon. Instead, the U.S.-China relationship will remain fragile and subject to miscalculation for decades to come.

However, it is important to again emphasize at the outset that Washington and Beijing, through sustained diplomacy, can manage this enduring intense policy contention in ways that avoid perpetual confrontation.[10] This would require thoughtful and prudent statecraft in both capitals, which is now not the case. Given the current dispiriting condition of the U.S.-China bilateral relationship, one could become defeatist regarding the likely outcome of their strategic competition. But as former Secretary of State George Shultz once stressed to colleagues in the U.S. State Department, pessimism is not an acceptable option for Washington policymakers.[11] Inspired by Shultz's determined conviction, this report offers a grand strategy with twenty-two policy prescriptions to defend U.S. national interests, stabilize the U.S.-China bilateral relationship, and promote world order.

CHINA'S GRAND STRATEGY

No nation in the history of the world has risen as fast as China with such regional and global reach.[12] Its ascent is astonishing. Winston Churchill understood the problem of a bureaucracy not coming to terms with a new strategic challenge: "When a flood comes, the water flows over the culvert whilst the pipe goes on handling its 3 inches. Similarly the human brain will register emotions up to its '3 inch limit' and subsequent additional emotions flow past unregistered."[13] U.S. policy toward the People's Republic of China (PRC) is now primarily carried out in Churchill's three-inch pipe, while the Chinese strategic flood continues. As former Singaporean Prime Minster Lee Kuan Yew observed, "The size of China's displacement of the world balance is such that the world must find a new balance. . . . It is not possible to pretend that this is just another big player. This is the biggest player in the history of the world."[14]

In that context, Beijing seeks to:[15]

- replace the United States as the primary power in Asia;

- weaken and ultimately dissolve the American alliance system in Asia;

- undermine Asian nations' confidence in U.S. credibility, reliability, and staying power;

- use its economic power to pull Asian nations closer to PRC geopolitical policy preferences;

- increase its military capability to strengthen deterrence against U.S. military intervention in the region;[16]

- cast doubt on the U.S. economic, political, and societal model;

- ensure that U.S. democratic values do not diminish the Chinese Communist Party's hold on domestic power; and

- avoid a major confrontation with the United States in the next decade.[17]

U.S. GRAND STRATEGY TOWARD CHINA

In the face of China's long-term objectives and in the aftermath of the U.S. victory in the Cold War and the end of containment, U.S. policy-makers continue to struggle to conceptualize a grand strategy and derive and implement policies that would prove adequate to the nation's new circumstances, beyond the generic desire to protect the liberal international order underwritten by American power in the postwar era.[18] Though the U.S. Department of Defense during the George H.W. Bush presidency presciently contended that its "strategy must now refocus on precluding the emergence of any potential future global competitor"—thereby consciously pursuing the strategy of primacy that the United States successfully employed to outlast the Soviet Union—there was some doubt at the time whether that document reflected administration policy.[19] In any case, no administration in Washington has either consciously or consistently pursued such an approach, or formulated and implemented policies to that strategic purpose. To the contrary, a series of administrations conducted policies that enabled the rise of China, despite the fact that the original impulse for these policies—the containment of the Soviet Union—lost its justification with the demise of Soviet power.

Although China's history is marked by many times in which it had regional dominance but eschewed power elsewhere, this era is different. It is characterized by Beijing's growing nationalism and self-confidence, as well as its unprecedented involvement in the international system and its consequential decisive effects on China's internal stability, beginning with the global economy. In this context, Lee Kuan Yew emphasized:

> Why not? They have transformed a poor society by an economic miracle to become now the second-largest economy in the world—on track, as Goldman Sachs has

predicted, to become the world's largest economy. . . . They have followed the American lead in putting people in space and shooting down satellites with missiles. Theirs is a culture 4,000 years old with 1.3 billion people, many of great talent—a huge and very talented pool to draw from. How could they not aspire to be number 1 in Asia, and in time the world?[20] . . . It is China's intention to be the greatest power in the world.[21]

Not recognizing the clarity of Lee's analysis and conclusions, successive U.S. administrations spoke routinely about a strategic partnership with China, pursued an "engage and hedge" strategy vis-à-vis China, and profoundly misread Beijing's strategic intentions.

A 1997 statement issued at the summit between U.S. President Bill Clinton and Chinese President Jiang Zemin observed that

while China and the United States have areas of both agreement and disagreement, they have a significant common interest and a firm common will to seize opportunities and meet challenges cooperatively, with candor and a determination to achieve concrete progress. . . . The two Presidents are determined to build toward a constructive strategic partnership between China and the United States through increasing cooperation to meet international challenges and promote peace and development in the world.[22]

At a 2001 joint press conference with Jiang Zemin, President George W. Bush said that "today's meetings convinced me that we can build on our common interests. . . . We seek a relationship that is candid, constructive, and cooperative."[23]

In a joint press conference with President Xi Jinping in 2015, President Barack Obama noted that "as a result of our efforts, our two nations are working together more closely across a broader range of critical issues—and our cooperation is delivering results, for both our nations and the world."[24] Obama told the *Atlantic*'s Jeffrey Goldberg, "I've been very explicit in saying that we have more to fear from a weakened, threatened China than a successful, rising China."[25] Unfortunately, Beijing is busy proving him wrong.

While these forthcoming statements were being issued from the White House at various times, Beijing rejected the principle of reciprocity in the bilateral relationship, and Washington did next to nothing; stole billions of dollars of U.S. intellectual property, and Washington did next to nothing; manipulated its currency to the disadvantage of the United States, and Washington did next to nothing; mounted cyber penetration of U.S. infrastructure and critical facilities, and Washington did next to nothing; conducted widespread influence campaigns within the United States, and Washington did next to nothing; used coercion to obtain the advanced technology of U.S. companies in China, and Washington did next to nothing; threatened U.S. allies and partners in the Indo-Pacific, and Washington did next to nothing; used its enormous geoeconomic resources to pressure its neighbors and beyond, and Washington did next to nothing; systematically increased its autocratic influence in international organizations, and Washington did next to nothing; and built and militarized artificial islands in the South China Sea, and Washington did next to nothing.

Washington's guileless approach to China continued long after Beijing's international misbehavior had accelerated under Xi Jinping, and when hedging should have changed into much stronger and more decisive action to counter China's threats to U.S. vital national interests.[26] History is filled with such dangerous, even fatal, miscalculations, going back to the Romans, the Greeks, the Egyptians, the Chinese, and earlier.[27]

These U.S. misunderstandings of China's objectives over nearly two decades rank as one of the three most damaging U.S. foreign policy errors since the end of World War II, along with the 1965 military escalation in Vietnam and the 2003 invasion of Iraq. Indeed, this prolonged failure in China policy could turn out to be the biggest U.S. policy deficiency in the past seven decades, given the accumulating dangerous strategic consequences of the rise of Chinese power for world order, as well as for the United States and its allies, partners, and friends.[28]

The United States has just entered the fourth phase of its relationship with China since the end of World War II. In phase one, Mao Zedong's decision to go to war with the United States in Korea in 1950 produced a long period of antagonistic interaction. Phase two saw Richard M. Nixon and Henry Kissinger open up the relationship to better meet the global Soviet threat and, they hoped, help end the Vietnam War on honorable terms. In phase three, Washington sought to bring Beijing ever more into the international system, hoping it would eventually become a "responsible stakeholder" and accede to U.S.-fashioned rules of domestic and international order.[29] Now in phase four, the United States is beginning to fully digest the aggressive elements of Chinese power projection and take initial actions to deal with it. To its credit, the Donald J. Trump administration recognizes in its public statements the enormous challenges that the rise of China presents to the United States. It thus has a critical attitude toward China, but no grand strategy and no comprehensive and integrated work plan to implement that strategy. Trump himself veers from alpha to omega and back again on the subjects of China, and of Xi Jinping, and the sustained negative effects of the president's careening tweets on the Chinese leadership will likely last well beyond his time in office.

It was not inevitable that the U.S.-China relationship would evolve into its current adversarial standoff. If Washington, through careful and consistent diplomacy in coordination with its Asian and European allies, had routinely contested Beijing's aggressive policies much earlier, China, then weaker, could have pulled back and a rough equilibrium could have been established and maintained, with major areas of cooperation. And if Beijing instead had continued on that confrontational path, Washington would have been in a stronger position to respond than it is at present. But the Chinese leadership, faced with successively acquiescent U.S. administrations that miscalculated China's strategic objectives, went on pushing until it finally provoked the current rhetorical Thermidorean reaction from the United States.[30]

Because U.S. efforts to "integrate" China into the liberal international order generated new threats to U.S. leadership in Asia—and produced a consequential challenge to American power globally—the United States requires a new grand strategy toward China. It should reverse the decline in U.S. standing and influence in Asia; balance with allies and partners the rise of Chinese power; promote Western values; and initiate a strategic dialogue with China to manage issues of dispute and seek areas of bilateral and international cooperation. This strategy cannot be built on a bedrock of containment, as was the earlier effort to limit Soviet power, because of the current realities of globalization.[31] Nor can it entirely jettison the policy of the PRC's integration into the international system, not least because of the intertwined character of the global economy. Rather, Washington should launch an all-out effort to limit the dangers that Beijing's economic, diplomatic, technological, and military expansion pose to U.S. interests in Asia and globally.

The twenty-two policy prescriptions in this report constitute the heart of an alternative balancing strategy. They derive from the clear recognition that to preserve a crucial U.S. role in shaping the global system remains the central objective of U.S. grand strategy in the twenty-first century. To sustain this status in the face of rising Chinese power entails several critical elements: revitalizing the U.S. economy to nurture those disruptive innovations that bestow on the United States asymmetric economic advantages over others and training a next-generation work force; creating new preferential trading arrangements among U.S. allies and partners to increase their mutual gains through instruments that consciously exclude China; reestablishing a technology-control regime that involves U.S. allies to prevent China from acquiring military and strategic assets that enable it to inflict "high-leverage strategic harm" on the United States and its partners; building up the power capacities of U.S. allies and partners on China's periphery; improving the means of U.S. military forces to effectively and promptly project power along the Asian rimlands and along vital sea lanes despite any Chinese opposition; and promoting American political, economic, and societal values in the international system—all while working with China in ways that promote U.S. national interests.

The necessity for such a balancing strategy—one that deliberately incorporates elements that limit China's capacity to misuse its growing power, even as the United States and its allies continue to interact with China diplomatically and economically—is driven by the fact that the likelihood of a long-term strategic rivalry between Washington and Beijing is high. China's sustained economic success over the past thirty-odd years has enabled it to aggregate formidable power, making it the nation most capable of dominating the Asian continent and thus undermining the traditional U.S. geopolitical objective of ensuring that this arena remains free of hegemonic control. The meteoric growth of the Chinese economy, even as China's per capita income remains behind that of the United States, provides Beijing with the resources necessary to challenge both the security of its neighbors and

Washington's influence in Asia, with potential perilous consequences. Even as the increase in China's overall gross domestic product (GDP) recedes, its relative growth rates are likely to be higher than those of the United States for the foreseeable future, thus making the need to balance its rising power indispensable. Only a fundamental collapse of the Chinese state would free Washington from the obligation of systematically balancing Beijing, because even the alternative of Chinese geopolitical and/or geoeconomic stumbles would not eliminate the dangers presented to the United States in the Indo-Pacific and beyond.[32]

There is no better basis to analyze and formulate U.S. grand strategy toward China than connecting that strategy directly to U.S. vital national interests—*conditions that are strictly necessary to safeguard and enhance Americans' survival and well-being in a free and secure nation*.[33] Note how exceedingly rigorous this definition of vital national interests is. Most foreign policy issues on the front page of the *New York Times* and in the media do not meet these definitional requirements. While others routinely claim that the United States has vital national interests from Syria to Yemen to Afghanistan to the South China Sea to Taiwan, only five vital U.S. national interests today are listed here, consistent with the austere definition above.

U.S. vital national interests are as follows:

1. Prevent the use and deter and reduce the threat of nuclear, biological, and chemical weapons and catastrophic conventional terrorist or cyber attacks against the United States, its military forces abroad, or its allies.

2. Prevent the use and slow the global spread of nuclear weapons, secure nuclear weapons and materials, and reduce further proliferation of intermediate and long-range delivery systems for nuclear weapons.

3. Maintain a global and regional balance of power that promotes peace and stability through domestic U.S. robustness, U.S. international power and influence, and the strength of U.S. alliance systems, with increased contributions from allies and partners.

4. Prevent the emergence of hostile major powers or failed states on U.S. borders.

5. Ensure the viability and stability of major global systems (trade, financial markets, energy supplies, the environment, and freedom of the seas).[34]

Instrumentally, these vital interests will be enhanced and protected by promoting U.S. leadership, military and intelligence capabilities, and credibility (including a reputation for adherence to clear commitments and evenhandedness in dealing with other states), and strengthening critical international institutions.[35]

These U.S. vital national interests, meant to safeguard and enhance Americans' survival and well-being in a free and secure nation, would be undermined by Chinese control in the Indo-Pacific. A China that dominated Asia could lead to nuclear proliferation across the region, beginning with Japan, as countries would seek a last-ditch nuclear deterrent capability. A China that dominated Asia could fatally fragment the United States' Asian alliance system, as one U.S. ally after another kowtowed to Beijing. A China that dominated Asia could undermine U.S.-Mexico ties in order to distract the United States from its Asian and global national interests. A China that dominated Asia would alter the values, rules, and practices of major international systems to U.S. disadvantage, beginning with global trade. In short, Odd Arne Westad has it right in a recent article in *Foreign Affairs*: "Like 70 years ago, to compete today, the United States needs to spend more money, which necessarily means higher contributions from wealthy Americans and corporations, in order to provide top-quality skills training, world-class infrastructure, and cutting-edge research and development. Competing with China cannot be done on the cheap."[36]

Chinese President Xi Jinping signaled China's aims to undermine the post–World War II Asian balance of power at the Conference on Interaction and Confidence Building Measures in Asia in early 2014 when he argued that "Asia's problems ultimately must be resolved by Asians and Asia's security ultimately must be protected by Asians."[37] The capacity of the United States to successfully address China's systematic geoeconomic, military, technological, and diplomatic challenge to U.S. leadership in Asia will determine the shape of the international order for decades to come.

THE CRITICS

Experts critical of this proposed grand strategy toward China fall into at least seven categories.[38]

First, some will argue that China has no grand strategy.[39] But although there are those in Beijing who disagree with Xi's current strategic approach, its dominating elements are not a mystery. Chinese officials insistently argue that the U.S. alliance system in Asia is a product of the Cold War and should be dismantled; that the United States' Asian allies should loosen their U.S. ties and that failure to do so will inevitably produce a negative PRC reaction; that U.S. efforts to maintain its presence and power in Asia are dimensions of an American attempt to contain China and therefore should be condemned and resisted; that U.S. military power projection in the region is dangerous and should be reduced (even as the People's Liberation Army [PLA] continues to build up its military capabilities with the clear objective of reducing U.S. military options in the context of a U.S.-China confrontation); and that the U.S. economic and political model is fundamentally exploitative and should have no application in Asia.[40] To not take seriously official Chinese government statements along these lines is to not take China seriously. That Beijing does not hope to realize these policy goals in the short term does not reduce their potential undermining effect in the decades ahead. In short, if China were to achieve the policy objectives contained in these official statements, it would clearly replace the United States as Asia's leading power. If that does not represent a PRC grand strategy, it is unclear what would.

Henry Kissinger in *A World Restored* is helpful in this regard:

> For powers long accustomed to tranquillity and without experience with disaster, this is a hard lesson to come by.

Lulled by a period of stability which had seemed permanent, they find it nearly impossible to take at face value the assertion of the revolutionary power that it means to smash the existing framework. The defenders of the status quo therefore tend to begin by treating the revolutionary power as if its protestations were merely tactical; as if it really accepted the existing legitimacy but overstated its case for bargaining purposes; as if it were motivated by specific grievances to be assuaged by limited concessions. Those who warn against the danger in time are considered alarmists; those who counsel adaptation to circumstance are considered balanced and sane, for they have all the good "reasons" on their side: the arguments accepted as valid in the existing framework.[41]

Such is the mistaken view of those who ignore the evidence and argue that China poses no serious threat to vital American national interests.[42]

Second, some may say that the analysis and policy recommendations here are too pessimistic, based on a worst-case appraisal of Chinese behavior. To the contrary, these conclusions are drawn from China's current actions regarding its internal and external security, its neighbors, and the U.S. presence in Asia. Nothing is projected that is not already apparent in Beijing's present policies and strategic intentions. Nevertheless, this hardly represents the worst case if China began to behave like the Soviet Union, necessitating something a great deal more far-reaching and costly than balancing.[43]

Third, others might argue that China's international behavior is "normal" for a rising power, that China is gradually being socialized into the international system, and that now is far too early for Washington to give up on comprehensive engagement and strategic reassurance toward Beijing. The issue is how long the United States should pursue a policy toward China that is clearly not sufficiently protecting U.S. vital national interests. Kurt Campbell, former assistant secretary of state for East Asian and Pacific affairs in the Barack Obama administration and a leading influence on its China policy, has stressed, "We were always looking for deeper cooperation with China and attempts to have on-the-ground cooperation—for example, on aid or humanitarian support operations, we weren't able to bring about; in military-to-military relations, on the diplomatic agenda, on aid, we found it very difficult to get meaningful results."[44] Such has been the experience of every American administration in this century.

Fourth, some may assert that China's integration into the international system broadly serves important U.S. purposes, binds China to a rules-based system, and increases the costs to the PRC of going against it, and thus should transcend other U.S. concerns about China's internal and external behavior.[45] Attempts to integrate China into international institutions will continue, and the United States will accrue some benefits from that activity. However, basing U.S. grand strategy primarily on such Chinese global integration ignores the strategic reality that China has made far greater relative gains through such processes than the United States has over the past three decades, that China has accordingly bolstered its national power in ways that deeply threaten U.S. national interests in the long term, and that therefore the United States needs to understand this disturbing trend and respond with much more robust policies and power projection into Asia.[46]

Fifth, critics may assert that the United States' Asian allies and partners will never go along with the grand strategy outlined in this report. This concern seems to concentrate not on the merits of this strategic approach but rather on its reception in the region. In any case, what the allies want is not to cut ties with China but rather to have expanded U.S. capabilities in the Indo-Pacific, bolstered reassurance of American protection, and intensified U.S. support for their own economic growth and security. The grand strategy outlined here advances all these objectives. Indeed, the worry across Asia today is not that the United States will pursue overly combative policies toward China; rather, it is that Washington may not be up to the challenge of consistently and effectively dealing with the rise of China over the long term.[47]

Sixth, a familiar concern is that if the United States treats China as an enemy, China will become an enemy.[48] A declaration by more than one hundred prominent China and other foreign policy experts warned against "U.S. efforts to treat China as an enemy."[49] This worry is difficult to understand.[50] No U.S. administration in the past half century, including the current one, has treated China as an enemy.[51] Moreover, over a nearly twenty-year period while the United States sought a strategic partnership with China, Beijing implemented a grand strategy designed to undermine U.S.-Asian alliances, which has accelerated under Xi Jinping; used geoeconomic tools to coerce its neighbors and others, including more recently through the Belt and Road Initiative (BRI); violated international commercial practices, including by committing massive theft of U.S. intellectual property; manipulated its currency for trade benefits; threatened Taiwan with invasion; built up its military forces to push the United States beyond Japan and the

Philippines; constructed and militarized artificial islands in the South China Sea, in violation of international law; systemically and brutally violated the human rights of its own people; and patiently and incrementally built its power and influence with the strategic goal of replacing the United States as the primary power in Asia.[52] It seems clear who is treating whom as an enemy, or at least as a strategic adversary.

Seventh, the question arises regarding how China will respond to the U.S. grand strategy recommended here. There are risks of pursuing this grand strategy. One could certainly expect a strong Chinese reaction. But it is likely that Beijing would continue to cooperate with Washington in areas that it thinks serve China's national interests—on the global economy, international trade, climate change, counterterrorism, the Iranian nuclear weapons program, North Korea (which cannot be managed without Beijing's agreement), and Afghanistan. Put differently, a fit of pique by the Chinese leadership—hardly in China's strategic tradition—would damage its policy purposes and its reputation around Asia. In short, this strategic course correction in U.S. policy toward China would certainly trigger a torrent of criticism from Beijing because it would begin to systemically address China's goal of dominating Asia, but it would not end aspects of U.S.-China international collaboration based on compatible national interests.

Although there are risks in following the course proposed here, as with most fundamental policy departures, such dangers are substantially smaller than those that are building because of an inadequate U.S. strategic and diplomatic response to the rise of Chinese power.[53]

A WORK PLAN
Twenty-Two U.S. Policy Prescriptions to Implement U.S. Grand Strategy Toward China

If it is not to lose its strategic struggle with China in Asia and globally, the United States needs to develop, along with its allies and partners, an integrated grand strategy that competes with the PRC across many integrated domains—diplomacy, the global economy, defense, digital technology/artificial intelligence (AI), the cyber sphere, public information, and ideology. Although the Trump administration is the first to recognize the failed policies of the past toward China, it has developed no such grand strategy toward the country, and thus no integrated and detailed work plan.[54] This puts the United States at a major strategic disadvantage because China does have a grand strategy. It wants to replace the United States as the strongest and most influential power in Asia and beyond, and is currently implementing that plan with considerable success. Unfortunately, these PRC advances have been accelerated by the Trump administration. The president, since taking office, has made the United States the most erratic, unreliable, and destabilizing major power; undermined U.S. alliances across Asia and Europe; and set out to divide the American people along class and racial lines.[55] Thus many policy prescriptions that follow will await a new president.[56]

U.S. DOMESTIC POLICY PRESCRIPTIONS

1. *The United States should mobilize all instruments of its national power to skillfully manage its economy; modernize its basic infrastructure; reform its immigration system; reduce its entitlement spending; rehabilitate the structure and quality of its education system; and address the serious political, economic, and societal divisions within the country.*[57] The U.S. contest with China over

international power and influence is likely to be decades long; a prosperous and well-functioning United States is the first requirement to ensure that Washington is well positioned not to lose that competition. Nevertheless, there is no need for strategic defeatism. The United States certainly has the resources to seriously deal with its domestic weaknesses, if it has the political and societal will.[58]

2. *The United States should protect the integrity of its democratic institutions, both for the good of the nation and to offer a powerful alternative model to China's authoritarian archetype.* China's meteoric rise, coupled with its present economic and military strength, makes the "China model" a beguiling path for some developing countries. While the United States is right to invest increased time and money to actively challenge China, liberal democratic values will be less attractive overseas if the United States cannot successfully manage its own affairs.

    Washington should especially guard the country's rule of law, the free press, and fair elections. Trump's tweets targeting, among other things, the judiciary and justice system, Congress, the Federal Reserve Bank, the media, and U.S. election practices, as well as spreading deep-state conspiracy theories, obviously make this problem substantially worse.[59]

    The United States should rebuild confidence in its democratic institutions through domestic civic education.[60] Just 26 percent of Americans can name the three branches of the U.S. government.[61] Robust civic education also increases voter turnout, reduces school dropout rates, and correlates with increased community participation.[62]

    If U.S. citizens lose faith in their own democratic institutions, the appeal of China's despotic model could be more attractive internationally than U.S. freedoms. Washington should recognize that foreign and domestic policy are inextricably linked, and that when the United States' reputation as a democratic "city on a hill" is tarnished, it puts the United States in a weaker strategic position abroad.[63] John F. Kennedy was right when he said, in his first presidential debate with Richard M. Nixon, "If we do well here, if we meet our obligations, if we're moving ahead, then I think freedom will be secure around the world. If we fail, then freedom fails. The kind of country we have here, the kind of society we have, the kind of strength we build in the United States will be the defense of freedom."[64]

3. *The United States should, in a measured way and through a bipartisan consensus, educate the American people regarding the nature and duration of China's challenges to U.S. vital national interests and*

democratic values, but its rhetoric should not instigate a "red scare." The United States should transform its narrative regarding the China challenge from defensive crouch to confident world leader determined to outpace and retard Beijing's strategic momentum and to maintain an open Indo-Pacific, while stressing its goal of reaching a stable and productive relationship with China.[65]

4.   **The United States should build the greatest possible sustained collaboration between the executive and legislative branches to meet the China challenge.** President Trump, as well as Republicans and Democrats in Congress, should recognize that opposing well-founded efforts to combat the rise of China based on unrelated policy disagreements is a self-defeating response to the rise of Chinese power.

In coordination with an executive branch reallocation of military assets (see policy prescriptions 7 and 9), Congress should support a robust defense budget to reflect the need to strengthen U.S. power projection into Asia and support for regional allies and partners.[66] The five-year $425 million Southeast Asia Maritime Security Initiative to help allies respond to Chinese naval activity is a good start, but it looks especially inadequate when compared to the trillions of dollars the United States has committed to efforts in the Middle East.[67] In addition, Congress should loosen restrictions on technology transfers to Asian allies and partners as well as develop new rules and schemes for cooperative technology development, especially with Japan.[68]

Congress was right to cooperate with the executive branch to create the U.S. International Development Finance Corporation (IDFC) as an alternative to China's BRI. To build on this effort, it should give the IDFC the freedom to quickly take advantage of opportunities when countries waver at the prospect of Chinese funding, and give the IDFC political support to fund riskier investments.[69] It should also support organizations like Radio Free Asia to better spotlight disturbing Chinese investments in the region.[70]

Additionally, Congress and the Trump administration should work together to properly fund and equip the Committee on Foreign Investment in the United States (CFIUS) to address national security concerns regarding Chinese investments.[71] They should also stress the importance of reviewing Chinese investments when speaking with counterparts in allied countries in Asia and Europe, and partners in Africa, Latin America, and the Middle East.

Finally, it would be naive to ignore Beijing's responses to Washington's shift of attention and funds toward the China challenge. For example, in the summer of 2018 China imposed tariffs on U.S. whiskey and cranberries.[72] Fruit and alcohol are hardly vital to U.S. national interests, but they are crucial to the economies of Kentucky and Wisconsin, the respective home states of Senate Republican Majority Leader Mitch McConnell and then Speaker of the House Paul Ryan.[73] Despite targeted pressure from Beijing, congressional leaders, including those who hold firm in their free-trade principles, should stand with the administration on dealing with Chinese power.[74]

5. *The United States should enact a technology control regime to limit China's theft of U.S. intellectual property.* China's cyber espionage is a threat to U.S. businesses, and Washington should punish Beijing for these aggressive cyber activities. But China has grown adept at getting what it wants via other means. Through financing chicanery and shell corporations with dubious claims of government independence, Beijing reportedly sought satellite technology from Boeing, the second-largest federal contractor in the United States.[75] Additionally, China is suspected of using joint ventures as a means for stealing U.S. chip technology from Micron and textile fibers from DuPont.[76] Considering that start-ups, with fewer resources than well-established corporations, are at the cutting edge of a range of new technologies, the need for a tighter technology control regime is all the more urgent.[77]

In order to strengthen domestic defenses against Chinese intellectual property theft, Washington should, through processes like those used by CFIUS, press for greater transparency on the part of foreign businesses that seek to invest in American enterprises. It should require that investors from nonmarket economies disclose their organizational structure and ties to military or government institutions before investing in U.S. ventures.[78] As the distinction between the Chinese government and Chinese private businesses becomes more difficult to discern, the United States will need to ensure that it does not accidentally cede technology to Beijing. Additionally, Washington should use its alliances to build a stronger front against China in this respect. Allied countries that possess similar laws of their own should join the United States in punishing China's infringements.[79]

But for American businesses, turning down Chinese investment, even when suspicious, may not be an easy proposition. Even if the national security concerns are clear to Washington, such worries do not guarantee they will be sufficient to convince a start-up to do without funds from the world's second-largest economy and a market of over one billion consumers.

In addition to activity designed to strengthen U.S. bargaining power against China in this domain, the United States should take steps to actively punish Chinese intellectual property coercion. To this end, the United States should use the broad powers of the International Emergency Economic Powers Act to punish entities shown to profit from forced technology transfers from U.S. firms and firms in U.S. allied nations. Such targeted sanctions would focus on specific perpetrators rather than the Chinese market as a whole, which, despite its myriad risks and problems, is crucial to U.S. enterprise.[80]

6. *Washington should launch a national private and public initiative to develop artificial intelligence (AI) technologies, robotics, quantum computing, semiconductors, and biotechnology in the military and civilian domains of government, the private sector, and academia.* This massive effort should be on the scale of the Manhattan Project, to acquire greatly increased capabilities for U.S. economic growth, quality of life, diplomacy, and algorithmic warfare. In cooperation with organizations like the recently created National Security Commission on Artificial Intelligence, regarding advanced machine reasoning, learning, and problem solving, the aim of these efforts should be to ensure that the United States does not lose the artificial intelligence race to China and thus allow China to shape AI ethical norms and technical standards for the decades ahead.[81]

To this end, Congress should substantially increase its funding for AI initiatives across government, education, and the private sector.[82] Proposed legislation calling for a $2.2 billion investment in AI research does not suffice when the city of Beijing alone apportions $2 billion to build an AI development park.[83] To meet the scope of this challenge, Washington should couple increased funding with interagency collaboration and adoption of AI technology.[84] The U.S. government is ideally positioned to invest in AI ethics, safety, and privacy—areas that do not promise private-sector profits—and should set aside funding with this in mind.[85]

Additionally, Washington should ensure that it maintains its lead in developing chips, which can be vital to AI research. Export controls preventing the sale of advanced chips to select Chinese firms, including the PLA-linked supercomputing company Sugon, are also useful.[86]

The United States should write clear and thorough regulations on AI and standards of liability to assuage private-sector uncertainty and promote safe and responsible applications of AI technology.[87] Though private tech firms can be fickle partners, they are crucial engines for American AI innovation. In December 2017, Google had as many as half of the world's top one hundred AI scientists.[88] If the United States is to come out ahead in AI competition with China, the private sector must do its part by collaborating on U.S. government projects and sharing intellectual property with the government when necessary to create more robust data sets and more effective applications.[89] If American tech firms take action similar to Google's decision to not renew its involvement with the Pentagon's Project Maven, U.S. AI strategy will be significantly undermined.[90]

The United States should ensure that it remains the top destination for cutting-edge AI talent.[91] Steps to this end should include a new National Defense Education Act that would fund up to thirty thousand scholarships in science, technology, engineering, and mathematics (STEM) to cultivate domestic research.[92] Washington should encourage immigration for AI researchers by allowing graduates from U.S. advanced STEM degree programs to receive a green card and make it easier, rather than harder, to work or study in the United States.[93]

Underlying the urgency of this U.S. effort is the reality that the global AI leader will likely set rules for AI technical standards, ethics, and governance.[94] The United States should take an active role in writing robust AI standards through the National Institute of Standards and Technology (NIST) and be present when international organizations discuss AI rules and practices.[95] Washington should also work with allies to develop agreed rules on the controversial topics of surveillance and lethal applications of AI, and it should work to establish enforcement mechanisms through groups like the International Organization for Standardization.[96] If China articulates the rules that govern AI, its companies could reap financial benefits and its government could set benchmarks and definitions to which the United States would have to adapt.[97]

U.S. INTERNATIONAL POLICY PRESCRIPTIONS

7. **The United States should not be diverted from the China question by regional problems around the globe.**[98] Beijing recognizes that one of its great advantages in this strategic competition is how much time and attention Washington spends on challenges elsewhere. U.S. decisions based on diplomatic, economic, military, and regional information and decision policy silos are particularly dangerous in the comprehensive context of the rise of Chinese power. Although, of course, the United States has vital national interests in other parts of the world, a large sign that says "Think China" should be placed on

the wall of the White House situation room. Such an ever-present reminder would hopefully move the discussion not just to U.S.-China bilateral issues but also to the question of how virtually every U.S. foreign policy decision affects U.S. efforts to deal with China. Beijing is increasing its power and influence in every area of the world, with enormous economic resources behind its often coercive policies—in Northeast Asia,[99] Southeast Asia,[100] South Asia,[101] the South Pacific,[102] Central Asia,[103] the greater Middle East,[104] Russia,[105] Europe,[106] Latin America,[107] Africa,[108] and the Arctic.[109]

An American president who understood the China challenge would not weaken U.S. prestige and reliability around the globe.[110] An American president who understood the China challenge would not withdraw from the Iran nuclear agreement with no consultation with allies, and with no clear strategy for next steps. An American president who understood the China challenge would not allow China to take the lead on international efforts to combat climate change. An American president who understood the China challenge would not threaten to bring U.S. troops home from Japan and South Korea. An American president who understood the China challenge would not pull the United States from the Trans-Pacific Partnership (TPP), again with no consultation. An American president who understood the China challenge would not provoke trade dispute after trade dispute with the closest allies of the United States, at a time when allied solidarity is an indispensable requirement to deal successfully and peacefully with a rising China.

An American president who understood the China challenge would not make deals with dictators at the expense of U.S. allies and continually disparage democratic heads of government. An American president who understood the China challenge would not stand by passively, or worse, while China increases its power and influence and promotes its autocratic model in international organizations. An American president who understood the China challenge would ask whether ever-closer China-Russia relations are consistent with U.S. national interests.[111] An American president who understood the China challenge would question, when Russia annexed Crimea in 2014, whether Washington should rush to impose long-term sanctions against Moscow, thus helping drive Russia toward an alliance with China. An American president who understood the China challenge would not permit administration officials to publicly cheer on the 2014 revolution in Kyiv, thus helping to confirm in Beijing (and Moscow) that the United States wants regime change in China. And an American president who understood the China challenge would do everything possible to concentrate on diplomacy and avoid attacking Iran, thus potentially triggering the United States' third long war since 2001.

8.   *Washington should intensify its diplomatic, economic, and security ties with its allies and partners in Asia and Europe.* The United States cannot successfully compete with China over the long term as a solitary actor, a unilateralist. It needs Asian and European allies, partners, and friends.[112] This will require: a recognition that these nations do not wish to be forced to choose between their economic interests regarding China and their security underpinnings provided by the United States; an alteration in the U.S. approach from dominating nation to more accommodating interlocutor; more intense consultation with others before Washington makes decisions, especially with respect to China; and a greater willingness to take the national interests of allies into account (including mediating the current dispute between Japan and South Korea).[113]

In short, the United States has to fundamentally reform the way it deals with its treaty allies and partners. No longer can Washington rely on its global and regional dominance to get its way. No longer can the United States ignore the views of important like-minded states and still achieve policy success. No longer can the United States avoid substantial compromise if it wishes to bring others along with its diplomatic preferences. It is difficult to exaggerate the fundamental change of mind and practice that will be required in Washington to implement this revolutionary approach toward U.S. allies and partners. In this context, it is crucial to remember that China has only two allies, North Korea and Pakistan, both of which are problematic.[114] The United States has an enormous advantage in this regard, but one that Trump persistently undermines. It is unclear how long it will take the next president to reestablish trust among U.S. allies, but it is unlikely to be rapid. As Kissinger observes, "Confidence is a precious commodity. Once plundered, it must grow again organically; it cannot be restored simply by an act of will or on the claim of national security."[115]

9.   *The United States should substantially strengthen its military power projection into Asia, shifting resources from the European and Middle Eastern theaters to improve the capability of U.S. military forces to effectively bring its power to bear within the first and second island chains despite any Chinese opposition.*[116] The United States needs more frequent and formidable naval activities, more

robust air force deployments, and more capable expeditionary for-mations—as well as greater partner capacity—to reinforce its preem-inent role in preserving peace and stability in Asia. This would include moving continental U.S. force structure to the West Coast (which is politically difficult because of local revenue and associated jobs) and more aggressive forward basing in Asia to avoid the higher number of rotational forces needed. Such actions will allow the United States not only to conduct increased activity with allies and like-minded partners and demonstrations of combat capability and freedom of navigation transits, but also to deter Chinese provocations, respond to regional crises, and reassure allies.

The United States in this context should take the following steps in concert with its Asian allies and partners:[117]

Japan. The United States should continue to work with Japan, Wash-ington's most important ally in the world and the cornerstone of U.S. strategy in Asia, to enhance the operational capabilities of the Japan Self-Defense Forces (JSDF). Indeed, without close and enduring U.S.-Japan security cooperation, it is difficult to see how the United States could maintain its present power and influence in Asia and compete successfully with China.[118] Japan has the third-largest global economy and an increasingly capable military, and it hosts fifty-four thousand American military personnel on its soil.[119] To bolster the U.S.-Japan alliance, the United States should:

- expand its security relationship with Japan, encompassing all of Asia;

- help upgrade the JSDF, including Japan's capabilities for joint, combined-arms, and expeditionary operations;

- align concepts such as *air-sea battle* and *dynamic defense* through a dialogue with Japan on roles, missions, and capabilities;

- reinvigorate an extended deterrence dialogue with Japan;

- intensify ballistic missile defense (BMD) cooperation with Japan;

- bring Japan into the Five Eyes intelligence sharing agreement;[120]

- establish combined U.S.-Japan Command and Control centers;

- enhance cooperation in anti-submarine warfare;

- pursue advanced space capability cooperation;

- revamp cooperative research and development and coproduction agreements;

- signal more often that Japan remains fully and reliably under the U.S. security umbrella;

- work with Tokyo and Seoul to reduce disagreements in their bilateral relationship;[121] and

- support Japan's cooperation with Australia, India, Vietnam, and other nations concerned with the rise of Chinese power.

South Korea. The linchpin of the United States' relationship with South Korea is their shared commitment to defending the latter from North Korean aggression. In that regard, the United States should promote stability on the Korean Peninsula. It should:

- boost the credibility of U.S.-extended nuclear guarantees to South Korea;

- ensure that adequate U.S. military capabilities are present on the Korean Peninsula in the context of provocations from North Korea;

- increase support for South Korea's BMD capabilities;

- keep Seoul fully informed regarding Washington's negotiations with Pyongyang;[122]

- formulate with Seoul a shared vision for dealing with Korean unification; and

- work with Seoul and Tokyo to reduce disagreements in their bilateral relationship.[123]

Australia. Australia is a crucial component of the United States' Indo-Pacific strategy. The United States should work with Australia to:

- hold more, and more frequent, deployments of U.S. military assets in the region;

- accelerate cyber, space, and undersea cooperation with Australia;

- more rapidly identify potential Australian contributions to ballistic missile defense; and

- support Australia's efforts to expand its strategic interaction with like-minded Asian nations.

India. In the face of an increasingly assertive China, the United States benefits from the presence of a robust democratic power that is willing to and capable of independently helping balance China's rising influence in Asia.[124] The United States should:

- substantially loosen its restraints on military technology transfer to India;

- regard Indian nuclear weapons as an asset in promoting a balance of power in Asia;

- markedly increase U.S.-India military-to-military cooperation, especially between the two navies;

- systemically assist India in building maritime capabilities in the Indian Ocean and beyond, including through substantial technology transfer;

- vigorously support India's Act East policy to strengthen its power projection and influence into Southeast and East Asia; and

- abandon the idea that India will join an alliance with the United States, but craft and articulate the importance of a unique relationship that is short of an alliance yet enables closer information sharing and diplomatic and military cooperation.

Southeast Asia. Association of Southeast Asian Nations (ASEAN) members are a major target of China's geoeconomic coercion, not least regarding issues in the South China Sea. The United States should:

- push harder for meaningful defense reform within the Armed Forces of the Philippines to develop a full range of defense capabilities that would enable the government to deter and prevent intrusions on or possible invasion of Philippine territory;

- boost Indonesia's role in joint exercises and expand its scope, which symbolically indicates Jakarta's growing centrality to security in the Asia-Pacific, and gear military aid, training, and joint exercises with Indonesia toward air-sea capabilities;[125]

- help Singapore upgrade its current air force capabilities from F-16s to F-35s;

- encourage Malaysia to fully participate in the Proliferation Security Initiative, which it agreed to join in April 2014, and promote more active Malaysian involvement in combined exercises, domain awareness architectures, and the like;

- expand the scope of activities during the annual U.S.-Vietnam naval exercises to include joint humanitarian assistance, disaster relief, and/or search and rescue exercises, and make more frequent stops at the port at Cam Ranh Bay in the short term;[126] and

- establish strategic International Military Exchange Training (IMET) programs with Myanmar, with a focus on professionalizing the military, and continue to integrate the Myanmar military into, and expand its participation in, joint international military and maritime domain awareness exercises and maritime security cooperation.[127]

10. *Washington needs to push Beijing to accept strict reciprocity, which needs to encompass all dimensions of U.S.-China relations.* As distinguished sinologist Elizabeth Economy argues, "Reciprocity has long been resisted by U.S. policymakers as precipitating a race to the bottom. However, when diplomatic and multilateral efforts fail, it should be a viable option. . . . There is little advantage to the United States in retaining its openness to Chinese influence, whether economic or political, if China is increasingly closing its door to the United States."[128]

In this spirit, Washington should continue to confront Beijing on its trade violations, which have been enduring and significant.[129] China subsidizes state-owned industries, including its steel and aluminum companies, and the resulting overcapacity dramatically undercuts metals prices.[130] It refuses to grant market access to U.S. and other firms across most of its economy.[131] It steals U.S. intellectual property and advanced technology.[132] It forces foreign tech firms that want to operate and sell goods in the country to work directly with Chinese firms and give them access to their secrets.[133] It steals new technology from foreign firms inside China using cyber tools. According to cybersecurity firm CrowdStrike, China was "the most prolific nation-state threat actor during the first half of 2018" and "made targeted intrusion attempts against multiple sectors of the economy, including biotech, defense, mining, pharmaceutical, professional services, transportation, and more."[134] These attacks have continued into 2019.[135]

Only the immediate fear of stringent U.S. retaliation will persuade Beijing to begin to cease its trade violations. As is obvious from more than two decades of Washington's policy failures, urbane U.S. diplomatic dialogue behind closed doors or public shaming on trade issues will not do what is necessary.[136] At the same time, it is unrealistic to believe that China will fundamentally reform its domestic economy to meet U.S. preferences. The current bilateral trade dispute needs to be resolved soon, as one step in a long process of reforming Chinese trade behavior.[137]

II. *Washington should recognize that neither its public rebukes nor its private entreaties are likely to change China's domestic political, economic, and social policies and practices, including its brutal human rights record; and that to fruitlessly advocate for regime change in China would sharply accelerate the downward spiral in U.S.-China relations.* Getting the right balance in response to China's pervasive human rights abuses is not easy, given American values. Kissinger observes in *Diplomacy* that "no nation has ever imposed the moral demands on itself that America has. And no country has so tormented itself over the gap between its moral values, which are by definition absolute, and the imperfection inherent in the concrete situations to which they should be applied."[138] The U.S. debate regarding human rights and China will continue; the most recent explosive case is Hong Kong. Some U.S. supporters of the demonstrations that are occurring at the time of this writing—including members of Congress—urge on the protesters' confrontational tactics. These well-meaning Americans risk contributing to a violent tragedy in Hong Kong, a Tiananmen II, which would set back improvements in the U.S.-China relationship for years to come.[139] Put simply, Xi Jinping cannot accept a democratic outcome to the turbulence in Hong Kong. To do so would trigger similar protests in cities across China and threaten his hold on power. President Trump is right to exercise prudence in this situation, not least to avoid further Americanization of the protests—which has already begun, with attendant U.S. flags and the singing of "The Star-Spangled Banner" at the demonstrations.[140] Regarding Hong Kong, Trump's cautious instincts are better than those of most of his senior advisors and members of Congress.

12. ***Washington should recognize that the Hong Kong crisis will have major consequences for the future of Taiwan, which is the current international issue most likely to produce military conflict between the United States and China.*** U.S. policy toward Taiwan has been a major success: it has encouraged the development of democracy in Taiwan but also opposed Taiwanese independence, in order to avoid a crisis with China. However, this delicate policy balance may be difficult to maintain in the period ahead. With China's concept of "one country, two systems" dramatically shown to be a fraud in Hong Kong, Beijing now has no operational cross-strait political theory for unification. Instead it must rely on economic coercion or, if that fails, use force to bring Taiwan back into China.[141] Thus the situation regarding Taiwan is now more dangerous than in many decades.[142] With this context, the United States should act with caution regarding Taiwan. While it should strengthen Taiwan's defenses, including with the F-16 sale, Washington should strictly adhere to the One China policy; strongly counsel Taipei to take no steps toward independence; and not intensify its diplomatic interaction with Taipei. It should also stress to Beijing that the use of force against Taiwan would rupture U.S.-China relations.[143]

In no case should Washington lead Taipei to believe that the United States will come to Taiwan's defense if its provocations, including steps toward independence, produce a cross-strait crisis. It is also crucial to understand that the cross-strait military balance has fundamentally changed. In eighteen consecutive unclassified war games simulating U.S.-China military conflict over Taiwan, the United States reportedly has never prevented China from conquering the island, which profoundly calls into question the persuasiveness of U.S. deterrence on this issue in Beijing.[144] Since no American president will want to have to decide whether to go to war with China if the PRC uses force against Taiwan, adroit U.S. diplomacy with both Beijing and Taipei is crucial. The complexity of the Taiwan situation and the U.S. role in its defense demands more rigorous policy discussions and greater public awareness in the United States. In particular, it is far from certain that the

American people would support U.S. use of force in response to a Chinese attack on Taiwan.

13. ***The United States should respond to Chinese cyberattacks with stiff economic sanctions and with focused, proportionate offensive cyber operations.*** China presents a persistent cyber espionage risk and an increasing threat to U.S. core military and critical infrastructure systems, such as power grids and financial networks, as well as to the American private sector, as noted in policy prescription 5. China needs to pay a serious price for its brazen cyber activities.[145] So far, "U.S. policy still lacks a coherent approach to protecting critical digital assets outside of the government and, in most cases, relies on the voluntary participation of private industry."[146]

In order to deter further Chinese cyber aggression and in the context of convening a formal international cyber group of like-minded nations, Washington should join with allies and partners to attribute attacks and use targeted, personalized sanctions against perpetrators, as well as against firms benefiting from Chinese espionage.[147] Public statements and unenforced indictments are nowhere near sufficient to deter Beijing from cyberattacks that reportedly net billions of dollars in intellectual property, help the PLA develop next-generation combat aircraft, and grant access to data on U.S. government workers.[148] In 2018, the United States carried out coordinated efforts with allies to attribute and punish Russian cyberattacks.[149] This action followed the April 2015 imposition of U.S. Treasury sanctions for "malicious cyber-enabled activities," which have previously been used against Russia, Iran, and North Korea.[150] Washington should use these sanctions as a model to punish attributable Chinese cyber aggression.[151]

Additionally, Washington should continue the Trump administration's focus on strengthening offensive capabilities in cyberspace. The United States should make clear to Beijing that a Chinese attack that harmed civilians or affected critical infrastructure or financial systems would prompt a response proportional to "comparable physical attacks." Washington should also build upon the Trump administration's stated goal to "defend forward" against increasing cyber aggression.[152] Strengthening responses to cyberattacks does risk upsetting China and increases the cost of misattribution, but the damage accrued by inaction is already far too high.[153]

At the same time, Washington should seek to develop with Beijing agreed rules of the road regarding cyber conflict. The United States and China should attempt to concur on, or at least articulate each other's definitions and understandings of, terms including *defensive* and *offensive operations, cyberattack, cyber weapons,* and even *cyberspace,* for which no mutual understanding exists.[154] The two sides should formally pledge to avoid cyber activity that interferes with the operations of each other's critical infrastructure and banking systems.[155] Crucially, none of the prescriptions mentioned here, which will be difficult to achieve in any case, will be accomplished if the U.S.-China relationship continues to deteriorate.

14. ***Washington should ramp up efforts to counter Beijing's influence operations within the United States.***[156] This approach requires greater transparency at the start to prevent Beijing from exploiting the openness and accessibility of U.S. universities, think tanks, private organizations, businesses, and state and local governments. Beijing coerced U.S. airlines to scrub mentions of Taiwan as separate from China, allegedly hijacked once-legitimate Twitter accounts to push inflammatory viewpoints to American followers, and donated money to think tanks and universities to indirectly dissuade them from promoting views contrary to those of the Chinese government.[157]

In October, Houston Rockets General Manager Daryl Morey tweeted an image supporting the protests in Hong Kong. In response, Chinese internet company Tencent Holdings, which has a $1.5 billion streaming deal with the National Basketball Association (NBA), blacked out exhibition games; the Chinese government asked NBA Commissioner Adam Silver to fire Morey (Beijing has since denied Silver's claim); and Nike stores in China pulled Rockets merchandise from shelves.[158] That the championship-contending Rockets reportedly discussed the employment status of a general manager who won the 2018 NBA Executive of the Year award and is widely regarded as a pioneer of basketball analytics is a testament to China's influence.[159] Washington should support U.S. companies that resist such Chinese coercion.

China's United Front Work Department (UFWD), once a tool for influencing diaspora communities, has broadened its focus to include foreign-state and private-sector institutions of varying importance and prestige.[160] Prior to new rules enacted by the Trump administration, Chinese diplomats enjoyed wide-ranging freedoms in the United States while American diplomats in China ran into difficulties when they tried to meet with locals, travel abroad, or participate in events at Chinese universities.[161]

To address these issues, groups in the United States affiliated with Chinese United Front organizations should be made to register as agents of a foreign power under the Foreign Agents Registration Act.[162] To better defend against influence tactics and foster improved oversight, American universities should make public their agreements with Confucius Institutes, which are funded by the Chinese government, and should remove clauses requiring the institutes to operate "according to China's laws." Similarly, think tanks should publicly disclose funding sources and uses and strive to ensure that Chinese funders cannot influence or censor products or research topics.[163]

Though transparency in funding and government connections is a useful starting point, China's economic weight means American institutions often face tangible consequences for taking up positions contrary to Beijing's party line. Targeted organizations should collaborate with one another, which could produce greater awareness of China's influence efforts. American institutions, especially think tanks and universities, should publicize their difficulties conducting research related to China and share information with each other. As an additional measure, they should formulate a shared code of conduct to outline acceptable and unacceptable practices when dealing with analogous institutions in China.[164] Subnational governments, another frequent target of Chinese influence campaigns, should develop their own understanding of Chinese activities in their jurisdictions and run due diligence on members of visiting Chinese delegations.[165]

While Washington may want to dramatically reduce the effects of China's influence campaign in the United States, the openness of the American media landscape and the freedoms afforded U.S. news outlets allow Beijing to use China Central Television (CCTV)—a propaganda outlet of the Chinese Communist Party—to put party views on American airwaves.[166] To reduce the dissemination of Beijing's views throughout the United States, U.S. organizations with the capacity to do so should support independent Chinese-language media outlets through grants, cyber assistance, and other means. In addition, the Federal Communication Commission should investigate whether CCTV's dominant share of the Chinese-language cable news market in the United States is the result of unfair practices.[167]

15. **Washington should not seek a China-first approach to the region, since the United States requires its allies to compete with the PRC over the long term.** Such a Group of Two (G2) bilateral focus would suggest a great-power condominium that puts China, rather than the U.S. alliance system, at the center of U.S. strategy in Asia. In any event, a G2 focus has never been possible or advisable. China has too many

other important bilateral relationships, and the United States should never weaken its alliance systems or close partnerships through such a G2 arrangement. Further, the two countries, strong and influential as they are, cannot seriously address global problems such as the international economy, proliferation of weapons of mass destruction, energy, climate change, counterterrorism, and many others, over the long term without close coordination with dozens of other nations. Instead of a G2, the United States should embed its China policy within a larger Asia-wide framework, intensifying every one of Washington's other bilateral relationships in the region. To deepen and diversify contacts throughout Asia, beginning with allies, would allow the United States greater influence in the Indo-Pacific and generate greater capacity to shape China's external choices.

16. *Washington should develop a more robust economic presence in Asia and should work with regional partners to coordinate policies that counter Chinese geoeconomic coercion.*[168] While China's military has grown dramatically in recent years, it has avoided direct armed conflict in favor of using its economic strength as a tool to achieve geopolitical objectives.[169] A U.S.-led coordinated geoeconomic initiative is required to reduce China's capabilities to economically pressure other nations. This will not be easy. In part because it is the largest trading partner with U.S. allies Australia, Japan, and Korea, China has yet to face significant consequences for using geoeconomic policies as a tool to intimidate other nations into complying with Beijing's demands.[170] Such a strategy should expand free-trade areas and market access to reduce Beijing's economic centrality, provide alternatives to the BRI in strategically important areas, and increase economic and security cooperation to harmonize responses to Chinese coercion.

In addition, the United States should coordinate international investment strategies and campaigns with regional allies and partners to make available viable alternatives to Belt and Road funding in important areas. Countries in critical regions, such as Australia, India, and Japan in Asia and Saudi Arabia in the Middle East, should, with support from the United States and other donors, provide targeted grants and loans as an alternative to BRI. This effort should include public funding from government and multilateral aid agencies, as well as investment through the private sector. Japan's ability to provide high-tech, high-quality projects that employ more local workers and have lower interest rates than BRI should be a model.

To further strengthen regional cooperation among allies, the United States should ratify and expand multilateral trade deals that exclude China. Free trade agreements supply countries that might be vulnerable to Beijing's geoeconomic coercion with access to other markets, including the large U.S. market. As a step to this end, the United States should join the Comprehensive and Progressive Agreement for Trans-Pacific Partnership (CPTPP), formerly known as the Trans-Pacific Partnership. Washington should support such agreements, including Japan's recent trade agreement with the European Union.

In addition, the United States should join the Asian Infrastructure Investment Bank (AIIB).[171] Remaining on the sidelines will do nothing to assuage Washington's concerns about the bank's low environmental, credit, and governance quality controls, nor will it reduce China's 26.6 percent voting share.[172] By joining the group, the United States would keep U.S. businesses informed of AIIB activity and gain a platform to ensure that Beijing upholds Article 31 of the bank's articles of agreement. The article states that the AIIB, "its President, officers and staff shall not interfere in the political affairs of any member, nor shall they be influenced in their decisions by the political character of the member concerned."[173]

Finally, the United States should begin a consultation process among allies in Asia and Europe to identify geoeconomic vulnerabilities and to design resiliency and diversification efforts to address those vulnerabilities.[174] This should include reaching agreements that if one ally suffers economic coercion, another does not take advantage and fill in behind.

17. *The United States should marshal its diplomacy with nations within the region, as well as those outside it (e.g., European countries that favor rules-based approaches—although this will require awakening Europe from its strategic stupor), in order to strengthen international organizations to make progress on climate, free trade, international security, and freedom of navigation.*[175] This coalition of the democratic willing, this "global commonwealth," as President George H.W. Bush called it, should be launched at the heads-of-government level in Washington.[176]

18. *The United States, in coordination with allies, should attempt to initiate an extended conversation with Vladimir Putin and the Russian government on world order and the security of Europe and Asia.*[177] Zbigniew Brzezinski, in analyzing threats to the United States, warned that "the most dangerous scenario [would be] a grand

coalition of China and Russia . . . united not by ideology but by complementary grievances."[178] In particular, Russia would surely consider moving further into Ukraine in the event of a full-blown U.S.-China confrontation over Taiwan. Thus the increasing Russian embrace of China is clearly not in the U.S. national interest, and it would be useful to introduce in Beijing the idea that Russia's current bear hug may not be permanent.

As was the case during the Nixon-Kissinger opening to China, over the long term the United States should aim for a better relationship with both Russia and China than they have with each other. To be clear, Washington will have to make concessions in order to improve its relationship with Moscow; it cannot do so while retaining all its current policies toward Russia.[179] The same is, of course, true of Moscow. In that spirit, the United States should seek to negotiate an agreement with Russia in which North Atlantic Treaty Organization (NATO) enlargement is over and done, the United States lifts its sanctions against Russia regarding its annexation of Crimea, and Russia is readmitted to the G8. In return, Moscow would verifiably end its interference in eastern Ukraine through withdrawing its forces and agree to the deployment of a UN peacekeeping force, and stop its poisonous interference in U.S. politics and culture. (Since it is inconceivable that Moscow will ever withdraw from Crimea, do enthusiasts for those sanctions want them to stay in place in perpetuity?) The Arctic is a promising area for the United States and Russia to seek a more cooperative relationship based on research, safety of navigation, Arctic search and rescue, environmental response, or the plight of indigenous populations.

19. *Washington, in coordination with Asian allies, should negotiate with Beijing a joint initiative to present to Pyongyang regarding its nuclear weapons and ballistic missiles.* Recognizing that no agreement with North Korea will be possible without strong Chinese support, even coercion, the United States should drop its unrealistic insistence that North Korea now completely give up its nuclear weapons.[180] Instead, the United States and China should propose an interim agreement, beginning with a verifiable freeze on North Korean nuclear weapons tests and production and ballistic missile tests, in return for a modest reduction in economic sanctions.[181]

20. *The United States should, in coordination with allies and partners, initiate bilateral talks with China over the future of the South China Sea, with the aim of no further militarization of China's artificial*

islands and a strong mutual commitment to freedom of the seas, without prejudice to the final disposition of South China Sea sovereignty.[182] China has reclaimed over three thousand acres of land in the region; taken de facto control of Scarborough Shoal, despite a preexisting claim from the Philippines, a U.S. treaty ally; deployed anti-ship cruise missiles in the disputed Spratly Islands; and landed bombers on Woody Island, putting Manila in striking range.[183]

Beijing will not come to the negotiating table if the status quo holds, so Washington will have to signal privately that there will be costs for increased Chinese military activity in the region.[184] The United States should warn China that if it expands its efforts to reclaim land and deploy military assets, the United States will abandon its policy of neutrality on competing territorial claims in the South China Sea and aid targets of aggressive Chinese activity in the region. American assistance could include joint military exercises and provision of surveillance drones, mines, and anti-ship missiles to regional partners.[185]

The United States should collaborate with Australia, Japan, the Philippines, and Vietnam, as well as European allies, on patrols and other activities to demonstrate to China that a coalition of states is working to defend freedom of navigation. Further, the United States and its allies should increase their public opposition to Chinese activity in the South China Sea. Washington, with the support of its allies and partners, should use platforms including the G7 to make an explicit commitment to the lawful use of the seas and to uphold the economic rights of Southeast Asian nations within their respective exclusive economic zones.[186] If Washington expects Asian nations to agree to a tougher stance on Chinese activity in the South China Sea, it will have to increase its economic and diplomatic support for these countries. U.S. efforts to provide a viable alternative to Chinese economic investment are crucial to ensure the cooperation of allies fearful of the prospect of Beijing's economic coercion.[187]

21. *The United States should launch an urgent and comprehensive bilateral dialogue with China regarding climate change.*[188] Together, the United States and China are responsible for more than 40 percent of global emissions, and the world is suffering the effects.[189] A global climate plan that excludes the United States or China is futile. In the midst of the U.S.-China trade war and necessary efforts to compete with China in many domains, Washington should recognize that climate change is not a competition: it is a problem to be solved with robust bilateral dialogue and international collaboration. The United States

can and should adopt policies in cooperation with China to jointly reduce emissions and encourage the rest of the world to do the same.

The United States should rejoin the Paris Agreement. When the Trump administration withdrew from the agreement, China immediately became the de facto world leader for setting climate policy standards.[190] Rejoining the Paris accord would give Washington a mechanism to coordinate with allies to hold Beijing accountable for actions like its coal-fueled BRI infrastructure projects.[191] As a way of measuring the effectiveness of each other's climate initiatives, Washington and Beijing should create joint metrics to codify efforts to fight climate change and develop mechanisms to more accurately measure these activities. These metrics could take several forms, such as measuring physical emissions output, the financial cost of mitigation, or the price of greenhouses gases.[192]

In addition to withdrawing from the Paris Agreement, President Trump altered the U.S.-China Strategic and Economic Dialogue and the Joint Commission on Commerce and Trade in ways that shift focus away from environmental issues. In order to reopen avenues for climate dialogue, the United States and China should develop cooperative programs for domestic energy investments and trade in low-carbon technology and goods.[193] As Washington and Beijing hit each other with trade restrictions, the two sides should work to reduce tariffs on goods that are important to combating climate change, including carbon capture technology, where the two nations are not in direct competition.[194]

On a more competitive note, China hopes to serve as a source for alternatives to U.S. energy.[195] If the United States continues its withdrawal from climate policy organizations like the Paris Agreement and Mission Innovation, China will be influential in writing the rules of a range of climate initiatives, including energy finance, automobiles, and geoengineering—the concept of changing the earth to solve climate-related issues. The latter may sound like science fiction, but China has already experimented with artificial rain clouds on the Tibetan Plateau.[196] China could also set regulations to hamper the market for U.S. energy resources and turn clean Chinese energy into a more viable alternative—a carbon emissions tariff could put U.S. energy resources at a disadvantage to Chinese clean technology.[197]

In its current policy direction, the United States is foolishly allowing China to take the lead on regulating green energy financing, an enterprise expected to grow to over a trillion dollars in the next decades.[198] Clean energy, not coal or natural gas, is the future, and ignoring new technologies could make the United States reliant on

Chinese products and regulations.[199] On the consumer level, as the Trump administration actively rolls back automotive regulations, China, which aspires to eliminate internal combustion vehicles, could become the benchmark for automotive manufacturers around the world. While Ford and General Motors develop electric vehicles specifically for the Chinese market, auto manufacturers scramble for ways to make cars that meet both Trump administration and California emissions standards.[200] The United States is already the standard-bearer in a range of clean technology areas, but Trump administration policies could surrender that role to Beijing for batteries, solar, and other emerging energy sources.

Unfortunately, climate reform is highly unlikely while Trump is in office. However, precedent does exist for U.S.-China collaboration below the federal level. The Chinese National Development and Reform Commission (NDRC) cooperated with California, and in 2013 the two signed a memorandum of understanding on climate issues. California also assisted the NDRC as it piloted emissions trading systems, and it agreed to share information about carbon-reduction initiatives. In September 2019, former California Governor Jerry Brown launched the California-China Climate Institute.[201] China's climate policy does not need help from a United States that has withdrawn entirely from the issue, but if the two nations cooperate bilaterally on climate policies, they can work together globally to address the problem of climate change in ways that benefit each country's national interests.

22. *As Washington implements policies to deal with the threatening aspects of the rise of Chinese power and gives Beijing incentives for moderation through the policies enumerated above, it should also construct a plausible path of classic diplomacy with China that would seek to ameliorate the growing tension between the two countries.*[202] A supreme effort by both sides is necessary to avoid a situation of permanent confrontation. Although such extended exchanges at high levels between Washington and Beijing will not end adversarial competition between the two, which will likely last for decades, they could help avoid worst-case outcomes. At this writing, there is reason to doubt that either side at present is capable of mounting a serious strategic dialogue, but there is no alternative to trying.[203]

If Washington and Beijing do not stop the downward turn in the bilateral relationship and lurch into prolonged intense confrontation or even conflict, the American and Chinese people would be the first to pay the price of this policy failure. Most of the rest of the world would soon join the suffering. Negative consequences would emerge for the United States' and China's formidable domestic challenges and national economies. Effects on the global economy would be devastating. Tension would dramatically increase throughout Asia, since no country in that region wants to have to choose between the United States and China. The effect on potential U.S.-China collaboration on climate change and other issues of global governance would be deeply corrosive. Attempts to deal with the nuclear weapons program of North Korea and potentially Iran would fall apart.

An energized U.S.-China discourse should be candid and high level—no rows of officials trading sermons across the table in Washington or Beijing. Bureaucracies wish to say today what they said yesterday, and wish to say tomorrow what they said today. It is therefore inevitable that representatives from Washington and Beijing routinely mount bills of indictment regarding the other side. Instead, in restricted private exchanges, U.S. and Chinese leaders (not career officials) should, as indicated at the outset of this report, candidly address how the application of their countries' perceived national interests could be circumscribed to avoid U.S.-China confrontation, in what ways world order should be rebalanced, and what set of mutually accepted international rules and practices the two sides should use.[204]

Although both the United States and China will continue to make their respective positions clear in public pronouncements, that is not likely to narrow the serious differences between the two sides. Therefore, Henry Kissinger's very private discussions with Zhou Enlai in the early 1970s should be the model for talks to explore President Xi's great power initiative. As Kissinger notes in his book *On China*, from 1972 onward, "What we encountered was a diplomatic style closer to traditional Chinese diplomacy than to the pedantic formulations to which we had become accustomed during our negotiations with other Communist states."

Statesmen have to make choices; they cannot do everything. Time is the most valuable resource of government leaders, and this policy prescription would require them to devote more time and energy to the U.S.-China undertaking and less on some of their other responsibilities, whether transatlantic relations or the latest problems in the Middle East. But no international challenge is more important for the heads of government in Washington and Beijing to address urgently and intensively than the deteriorating quality of the U.S.-China relationship. For the two sides to conduct contentious business as usual in these corroding circumstances is myopic. It is also dangerous and morally wrong.

However, for an intensified high-level bilateral dialogue between Washington and Beijing to be fruitful, the United States should first clearly establish that it is enhancing its military, diplomatic, and economic power projection into Asia, intensifying interaction with allies, partners, and friends, and helping build up their economic and military strength. Successful diplomacy depends on deployable assets, and Washington needs to increase its assets along the lines of the policy prescriptions in this report. Nothing less will convince Beijing—which pursues classic realist policies based on the balance of power—that it has reasons, based on its national interests, to negotiate seriously with the United States. This will take some time, for Beijing will wait to see whether Washington becomes distracted and diverts its attention to other, lesser, issues in the daily headlines, as is its wont.

CONCLUSION

Some of these suggested policy proposals are familiar and have been debated in recent public discourse. Thus, prescriptive familiarity is increasingly not the problem with respect to U.S. policies toward China and Asia writ large. Rather, it is that most such efforts have seen too little connection to U.S. grand strategy, too little conceptual integration, too little policy intensity, and too little policy follow-through. As Leonardo da Vinci supposedly stressed, "I have been impressed with the urgency of doing. Knowing is not enough; we must apply. Being willing is not enough; we must do."[205]

ENDNOTES

1. This report draws on a paper prepared for the August 2019 meeting of the Aspen
    Strategy Group, as well as on Robert D. Blackwill, "Managing the U.S.-China Great
    Power Relationship" (presentation, World Cultural Forum, Shanghai, June 18, 2014),
    http://belfercenter.org/publication/managing-us-china-great-power-relationship;
    Robert D. Blackwill, "Indo-Pacific Strategy in an Era of Geoeconomics" (speech,
    Tokyo, July 31, 2018), http://cfrd8-files.cfr.org/sites/default/files/pdf/8-20%20
    Tokyo%20Presentation.pdf; Robert D. Blackwill, *Trump's Foreign Policies Are Better
    Than They Seem* (New York: Council on Foreign Relations, 2019), http://cfr.org
    /report/trumps-foreign-policies-are-better-they-seem; Robert D. Blackwill and Kurt
    M. Campbell, *Xi Jinping on the Global Stage* (New York: Council on Foreign Relations,
    2016), http://cfr.org/report/xi-jinping-global-stage; Robert D. Blackwill and Jennifer
    M. Harris, *War by Other Means: Geoeconomics and Statecraft* (Cambridge, MA:
    Harvard University Press, 2016); Robert D. Blackwill and Ashley J. Tellis, "The India
    Dividend: New Delhi Remains Washington's Best Hope in Asia," *Foreign Affairs*, http://
    foreignaffairs.com/articles/india/2019-08-12/india-dividend; and Robert D. Blackwill
    and Ashley J. Tellis, *Revising U.S. Grand Strategy Toward China* (New York: Council on
    Foreign Relations, 2015), http://cfr.org/report/revising-us-grand-strategy
    -toward-china. Some academic theorists are uncomfortable with the term *primacy*,
    arguing that it is an overly simplistic concept. *Merriam-Webster's Collegiate Dictionary*
    defines primacy as "the state of being first (as in importance, order, or rank)." That is
    good enough for me. Governments in the Indo-Pacific are less analytically rigorous
    than university scholars on the question of primacy. From 1945 to 2010, Asian leaders
    believed they knew what primacy meant—they cared more about what the United
    States thought and did than they did about any Asian power. For some of these nations,
    that is no longer the case. The loss of U.S. primacy and the rise of China affects how
    they act in the world every day.

2. Not all believe that China threatens U.S. leadership in Asia. For a thoughtful
    argument, with which I do not agree, along these lines, see Michael Beckley, "Stop
    Obsessing About China: Why Beijing Will Not Imperil U.S. Hegemony," *Foreign
    Affairs*, September 21, 2018, http://foreignaffairs.com/articles/china/2018-09-21
    /stop-obsessing-about-china; and his book *Unrivaled: Why America Will Remain the
    World's Sole Superpower* (Ithaca: Cornell University Press, 2018).

3. My views on this have evolved over the past several years as Chinese power has increased. I now conclude that U.S. primacy in Asia, despite my preference for it, is no longer possible for the foreseeable future. In light of primacy's decline as a viable option for the United States, a number of strategists call for a policy of "restraint," which often translates into a substantial U.S. withdrawal from international commitments and influence. I could not disagree more with their argument. Such U.S. restraint in the current era would lead to a world in which China exercised decisive power. See Beverly Gage, "The Koch Foundation Is Trying to Reshape Foreign Policy. With Liberal Allies," *New York Times Magazine*, September 10, 2019, http://nytimes .com/interactive/2019/09/10/magazine/charles-koch-foundation-education.html; Judah Grunstein, "Why Restraint Is Winning Over More of the U.S. Foreign Policy Establishment," *World Politics Review*, September 4, 2019, http://worldpoliticsreview .com/articles/28161/why-restraint-is-winning-over-more-of-the-u-s-foreign- policy-establishment; Stewart M. Patrick, "The Case for Restraint: Drawing the Curtain on the American Empire," *World Politics Review*, August 26, 2019, http:// worldpoliticsreview.com/articles/28150/the-case-for-restraint-drawing-the-curtain- on-the-american-empire; and Stephen Wertheim, "The Only Way to End 'Endless War,'" *New York Times*, September 14, 2019, http://nytimes.com/2019/09/14 /opinion/sunday/endless-war-america.html. For contrary views, see Ivo Daalder, "Commentary: Debunked! Most Americans Do Support the U.S. Engaging in World Affairs, not Retreating," *Chicago Tribune*, September 12, 2019, http://chicagotribune .com/opinion/commentary/ct-opinion-americans-support-nato-daalder-20190912 -ys3pj24jvbfjhhjjj6v4t43rxa-story.html; Richard Fontaine, "The Nonintervention Delusion: What War Is Good For," *Foreign Affairs*, November/December 2019, http:// foreignaffairs.com/articles/2019-10-15/nonintervention-delusion; and Robert B. Zoellick, "The Foreign Policy Americans Really Want," *Washington Post*, October 9, 2019, http://washingtonpost.com/opinions/the-foreign-policy-americans-really -want/2019/10/09/73073b60-eaa0-11e9-9306-47cb0324fd44_story.html.

4. A minority believe that is already the case, based on U.S. alliance relationships. See Phillip W. Reynolds, "U.S. Grand Strategy Is Alive and Well—The Evidence Is Happening All Around Us," *Small Wars Journal*, August 12, 2019, http:// smallwarsjournal.com/jrnl/art/us-grand-strategy-alive-and-well-evidence-happening -all-around-us.

5. In this respect, it is important to differentiate among U.S. treaty allies, who for decades have habitually followed the U.S. international lead; regional partners, who cooperate with Washington on a case-by-case basis; and friends, who generally wish the United States well but usually avoid contentious issues. All these relationships are important if the United States is to successfully and peacefully address the rise of China, and all are being undermined by President Trump.

6. There is an important book to be written on policies that the United States should formulate and implement in a world in which it no longer has primacy.

7. The most influential work on the danger of U.S.-China war is Graham Allison, *Destined for War: Can America and China Escape Thucydides's Trap?* (New York: Houghton Mifflin Harcourt, 2017).

8. As Sun Tzu put it, "When you surround an army, leave an outlet free." Sun Tzu, *The Art of War*, trans. Lionel Giles (Leicester: Allandale Online Publishing, 2000), 36, http://sites.ualberta.ca/~enoch/Readings/The_Art_Of_War.pdf. Henry Kissinger

agrees. In *Years of Upheaval*, he describes dealing with the parties during the 1973 war, stressing: "We had to appear implacable. But we also needed to show an honorable way out." Henry Kissinger, *Years of Upheaval* (New York: Simon & Schuster Paperbacks, 1982), 537.

9. Some analysts now wrongly argue that regime change in China must occur before the United States can deal successfully with the rise of Chinese power. See Joseph Bosco, "US Engagement Has Failed in China," *Taipei Times*, September 21, 2018, http:// taipeitimes.com/News/editorials/archives/2018/09/21/2003700833; Anders Corr, "Democratizing China Should Be the U.S. Priority," *Journal of Political Risk* 7, no. 7 (July 2019), http://jpolrisk.com/democratizing-china-should-be-the-u-s-priority; Aaron Friedberg, "Getting the China Challenge Right," *American Interest*, January 10, 2019, http://the-american-interest.com/2019/01/10/getting-the-china-challenge -right; Michael Mandelbaum, "In Praise of Regime Change," *Commentary*, February 2019, http://commentarymagazine.com/articles/in-praise-of-regime-change; and Henry Olsen, "This Is Why Trump Is Right to Challenge China," *Washington Post*, October 1, 2019, http://washingtonpost.com/opinions/2019/10/01/this-is-why-trump -is-right-challenge-china.

10. The tools of classic diplomacy are being consumed by the twenty-four-hour news cycle, social media, partisan and bureaucratic politics, and the diminishing quality of foreign policy staff work within the government. One worries that American diplomacy will eventually be taught in university classrooms the way Etruscan shards are examined today. As Kissinger explains in *Years of Renewal*, "Bureaucracies have grown so bloated that a large proportion—perhaps the majority—of documents deal with housekeeping or internal interagency disputes. They illuminate not so much geopolitical objectives or strategy as bureaucratic turf battles," and "Diplomats are more likely to be told what to say than why they should say it. Tactics and domestic politics substitute for strategy, and what strategy exists is confined to the minds of a few top policy-makers, who, fearful of leaks, rarely articulate or share it. History turns into an account of the immediate and sensational, devoid of historical perspective or long-term vision." Henry Kissinger, *Years of Renewal* (New York: Touchstone, 1999): 136, 138.

11. Shultz said this in a meeting I attended. It made a major and enduring impression.

12. For an extensive treatment of China's grand strategy, see Blackwill and Tellis, *Revising U.S. Grand Strategy Toward China*. See also Andrew Erickson, "Make China Great Again: Xi's Truly Grand Strategy," *War on the Rocks*, October 30, 2019, http:// warontherocks.com/2019/10/make-china-great-again-xis-truly-grand-strategy; Aaron Friedberg, "Competing with China," *Survival* 60, no. 3 (June/July 2018): 7–64, http:// tandfonline.com/doi/full/10.1080/00396338.2018.1470755; Melanie Hart and Blaine Johnson, "Mapping China's Global Governance Ambitions," Center for American Progress, February 28, 2019, http://americanprogress.org/issues/security/reports /2019/02/28/466768/mapping-chinas-global-governance-ambitions; Liu Mingfu, "'The World Is Too Important to Be Left to America,'" *Atlantic*, June 4, 2015, http://theatlantic .com/international/archive/2015/06/china-dream-liu-mingfu-power/394748; Bradley A. Thayer and John M. Friend, "The World According to China," *Diplomat*, October 3, 2018, http://thediplomat.com/2018/10/the-world-according-to-china; and Shinji Yamaguchi, "The Continuity and Changes in China's Perception of the International Order," *NIDS Journal of Defense and Security* 17 (December 2016): 63–81, http://www .nids.mod.go.jp/english/publication/kiyo/pdf/2016/bulletin_e2016_5.pdf.

13. As quoted in Max Hastings, *Winston's War: Churchill, 1940–1945* (New York: Alfred A. Knopf, 2010), 56.

14. Quote from Lee Kuan Yew in Nicholas D. Kristof, "The Rise of China," *Foreign Affairs*, November/December 1993, http://foreignaffairs.com/articles/asia/1993-12-01 /rise-china. Lee, along with Henry Kissinger, was the best-informed and most astute China watcher for forty years, and thus his views on the subject were prized by successive American presidents and other world leaders.

15. This articulation of China's goals was first published in Robert D. Blackwill, "China's Strategy for Asia: Maximize Power, Replace America," *National Interest*, May 26, 2016, http://nationalinterest.org/feature/chinas-strategy-asia-maximize-power-replace -america-16359. Not every Chinese strategist agrees with the PRC's aggressive objectives. After all, the U.S. alliance system arguably provides China with security; China presumably would not prefer a nuclear Japan in a full-fledged military alliance with India, Vietnam, etc. But Xi Jinping obviously sees things differently, as his foreign policy clearly demonstrates, and he is in charge.

16. Over the long term, China will not accept U.S. naval and air dominance in the Western Pacific. For details on PLA capability, see the Defense Intelligence Agency's *China Military Power* (Washington, DC: DIA Military Power Publications, 2019), http:// www.dia.mil/Portals/27/Documents/News/Military%20Power%20Publications/China _Military_Power_FINAL_5MB_20190103.pdf. Although the PLA military power projection has increased, some express skepticism regarding its effectiveness. See Dennis J. Blasko, "The Chinese Military Speaks to Itself, Revealing Doubts," *War on the Rocks*, February 18, 2019, http://warontherocks.com/2019/02/the-chinese -military-speaks-to-itself-revealing-doubts; Adam Ni, "Stronger but With Enduring Weaknesses: China's Military Turns 91," *RealClearDefense*, August 1, 2018, http:// realcleardefense.com/articles/2018/08/01/stronger_but_with_enduring_weaknesses _chinas_military_turns_91_113678.html; and Michael Peck, "Forget the Aircraft Carriers and Stealth Fighters: China's Military Is No Giant," *National Interest*, August 25, 2019, http://nationalinterest.org/blog/buzz/forget-aircraft-carriers-and-stealth -fighters-chinas-military-no-giant-75496. However, it seems beyond dispute that China would make intense efforts to ensure that the United States has no reasonable military options if Beijing uses force against Taiwan.

17. This is not to say that China's influence on the international system has been entirely negative in the past decade and a half. For its own strategic purposes, Beijing joined Washington in nonproliferation efforts regarding Iran and North Korea; reduced its carbon emissions; deployed 2,500 UN peacekeepers; and contributed more than any other country to global economic growth. But none of this balances China's encompassing efforts to replace the United States as the most powerful and influential nation in Asia, at the United States' expense.

18. Much of this chapter is reprinted with permission from Blackwill and Tellis, *Revising U.S. Grand Strategy Toward China*, and Blackwill, *Trump's Foreign Policies Are Better Than They Seem*. For a definitive administration view of the rise of Chinese power, see "National Security Strategy of the United States of America," White House, December 18, 2017, http://whitehouse.gov/wp-content/uploads/2017/12/NSS -Final-12-18-2017-0905.pdf; "Summary of the 2018 National Defense Strategy of the United States: Sharpening the American Military's Competitive Edge," Department of Defense, 2018, http://dod.defense.gov/Portals/1/Documents

/pubs/2018-National-Defense-Strategy-Summary.pdf; Mike Pence, "Remarks by Vice President Pence on the Administration's Policy Toward China" (speech, Washington, DC, October 4, 2018), http://whitehouse.gov/briefings-statements /remarks-vice-president-pence-administrations-policy-toward-china; Mike Pence, "Remarks by Vice President Pence at the Frederic V. Malek Memorial Lecture" (speech, Washington, DC, October 24, 2019), http://whitehouse.gov/briefings -statements/remarks-vice-president-pence-frederic-v-malek-memorial-lecture; and Mike Pompeo, "2019 Herman Kahn Award Remarks: US Secretary of State Mike Pompeo on the China Challenge" (speech, New York, October 30, 2019), http://s3.amazonaws.com/media.hudson.org/Transcript_Secretary%20Mike%20 Pompeo%20Hudson%20Award%20Remarks.pdf. For China's reaction to the October 24 Pence speech, see Chris Buckley, "China's Response to Pence Speech: 'Sheer Arrogance,'" *New York Times*, October 25, 2019, http://nytimes.com /2019/10/25/world/asia/china-pence-speech.html.

19.   "Excerpts From Pentagon's Plan: 'Prevent the Re-emergence of a New Rival,'" *New York Times*, March 8, 1992, http://nytimes.com/1992/03/08/world/excerpts-from-pentagon -s-plan-prevent-the-re-emergence-of-a-new-rival.html.

20.   Lee Kuan Yew, quoted in Graham Allison and Robert D. Blackwill, *Lee Kuan Yew: The Grand Master's Insights on China, the United States, and the World* (Cambridge, MA: MIT Press, 2013), 2.

21.   Lee Kuan Yew, "China's Growing Might and the Consequences," *Forbes*, March 28, 2011. See also Hal Brands, "China Is Determined to Reshape the Globe," Bloomberg, October 29, 2019, http://bloomberg.com/opinion/articles/2019-10-30/china-is -determined-to-reshape-the-globe.

22.   Bill Clinton and Jiang Zemin, "China-U.S. Joint Statement," Washington, DC, October 29, 1997, http://www.china-embassy.org/eng/zmgx/zywj/t36259.htm.

23.   George W. Bush and Jiang Zemin, "U.S., China Stand Against Terrorism" (joint press conference, Shanghai, October 19, 2001), U.S. Department of State, http://2001-2009 .state.gov/s/ct/rls/rm/2001/5461.htm.

24.   Barack Obama and Xi Jinping, "Remarks in Joint Press Conference" (joint press conference, Washington, DC, September 25, 2015), White House, http:// obamawhitehouse.archives.gov/the-press-office/2015/09/25/remarks-president-obama -and-president-xi-peoples-republic-china-joint.

25.   Jeffrey Goldberg, "The Obama Doctrine," *Atlantic*, April 2016, http://theatlantic.com /magazine/archive/2016/04/the-obama-doctrine/471525.

26.   For discussions of the "engage and hedge" strategy, see John Pomfret, "The Pendulum of U.S.-China Relations Is Swinging Again," *Washington Post*, September 11, 2019, http://washingtonpost.com/opinions/2019/09/11/pendulum-us-china-relations-is -swinging-again, and Jonathan D. T. Ward, *China's Vision of Victory* (Fayetteville, NC: The Atlas Publishing and Media Company, 2019).

27.   Pharaoh clearly did not sufficiently take into account Moses's strategic and tactical assets, in this case his god, as he led the Israelites out of captivity in Egypt and into the land of Canaan. The Egyptian intelligence community's failure regarding collection, collation, evaluation, analysis, integration, and interpretation reportedly cost Pharaoh his entire army and all its equipment in the Red Sea.

28. For a hypothetical about the consequences of this policy failure, see James Holmes, "World War II Teaches Us How World War III Could Happen (and Would Be Hell)," *National Interest*, September 1, 2019, http://nationalinterest.org/blog/buzz/world-war-ii-teaches-us-how-world-war-iii-could-happen-and-would-be-hell-77306.

29. Robert Zoellick, "Whither China? From Membership to Responsibility" (speech, New York, September 21, 2005), http://ncuscr.org/sites/default/files/migration/Zoellick_remarks_notes06_winter_spring.pdf. Zoellick is often misquoted. Contrary to some commentary on Zoellick's remarks, he expressed an unrealized objective regarding China's policy, not an assertion that Beijing had already become a "responsible stakeholder." For a thoughtful reflection on the history and consequences of the failed U.S. strategy toward China, see Hal Brands, "Every President Since Reagan Was Wrong About China's Destiny," Bloomberg, July 23, 2019, http://bloomberg.com/opinion/articles/2019-07-23/every-president-since-reagan-was-wrong-about-china-s-destiny.

30. For an example of a near consensus in Washington, David Brooks of the *New York Times* describes China as "an existential threat for the 21st century." David Brooks, "How China Brings Us Together," *New York Times*, February 14, 2019, http://nytimes.com/2019/02/14/opinion/china-economy.html.

31. For arguments against a policy of "neo-containment," see Kurt Campbell and Jake Sullivan, "Competition Without Catastrophe: How America Can Both Challenge and Coexist With China," *Foreign Affairs*, September/October 2019, http://foreignaffairs.com/articles/china/competition-with-china-without-catastrophe. The question does arise whether the United States should actually pursue a policy of containing China, while denying it is doing so. China seems convinced that is the current U.S. policy, whatever Washington says.

32. There is an impressive literature on China's many domestic weaknesses. For China's major demographic challenges, see Charlie Campbell, "China's Aging Population Is a Major Threat to Its Future," *Time*, February 7, 2019, http://time.com/5523805/china-aging-population-working-age; Anthony Fensom, "Dangerous Demographics: China's Population Problem Will Eclipse Its Ambitions," *National Interest*, September 16, 2019, http://nationalinterest.org/print/feature/dangerous-demographics-chinas-population-problem-will-eclipse-its-ambitions-80961; and Yi Fuxian, "Worse Than Japan: How China's Looming Demographic Crisis Will Doom Its Economic Dream," *South China Morning Post*, January 4, 2019, http://scmp.com/comment/insight-opinion/asia/article/2180421/worse-japan-how-chinas-looming-demographic-crisis-will. For China's many other domestic problems, see Lee Kuan Yew's enumeration in Allison and Blackwill, *Lee Kuan Yew*, 7–11; James T. Areddy, "China's Economy Shows Fresh Signs of Weakness," *Wall Street Journal*, June 16, 2019, http://wsj.com/articles/chinas-economy-shows-fresh-signs-of-weakness-11560512903; Keith Bradsher, "China's Economic Growth Hits 27-Year Low as Trade War Stings," *New York Times*, July 14, 2019, http://nytimes.com/2019/07/14/business/china-economy-growth-gdp-trade-war.html; Chris Buckley, "2019 Is a Sensitive Year for China. Xi Is Nervous," *New York Times*, February 25, 2019, http://nytimes.com/2019/02/25/world/asia/china-xi-warnings.html; Charles Burton, "Xi Jinping May Want to Rule the World, but He Has Problems at Home, Too," *Globe and Mail*, August 13, 2019, http://theglobeandmail.com/opinion/article-xi-jinping-may-want-to-rule-the-world-but-he-has-problems-at-home; Anna Fifield, "Paramount and Paranoid: China's Xi Faces a Crisis of Confidence,"

Washington Post, August 3, 2019, http://washingtonpost.com/world/asia_pacific
/paramount-and-paranoid-chinas-xi-faces-a-crisis-of-confidence/2019/08/02
/39f77f2a-aa30-11e9-8733-48c87235f396_story.html; George Friedman, "The Hong
Kong Extradition Bill and China's Weakness," Geopolitical Futures, June 18, 2019,
http://geopoliticalfutures.com/the-hong-kong-extradition-bill-and-chinas-weakness;
Yoko Kubota and Chao Deng, "China Faces Limited Options for Retaliating Against
Latest U.S. Threat," *Wall Street Journal*, August 2, 2019, http://wsj.com/articles/china
-faces-limited-options-for-retaliating-against-latest-u-s-threat-11564750795; Richard
McGregor, *Xi Jinping: The Backlash* (Australia: Penguin Random House, 2019), http://
sinocism.com/p/excerpt-from-xi-jinping-the-backlash; Karine Lisbonne-de Vergeron,
"China's Strengths and Weaknesses," Fondation Robert Schuman, April 4, 2012,
http://robert-schuman.eu/en/european-issues/0235-china-s-strengths-and-weaknesses;
Joseph S. Nye, "Commentary: China a Country With Great Strengths, but Also
Important Weaknesses," Channel News Asia, April 12, 2019, http://channelnewsasia
.com/news/commentary/china-us-rivalry-cooperation-strengths-weaknesses
-11424970; Joseph S. Nye Jr., "Does China Have Feet of Clay?" *Project Syndicate*,
April 4, 2019, http://project-syndicate.org/commentary/five-key-weaknesses-in-china
-by-joseph-s--nye-2019-04; Gordon Orr, "What Can We Expect in China in 2019?"
McKinsey & Company, December 2018, http://mckinsey.com/featured-insights/china
/what-can-we-expect-in-china-in-2019; Minxin Pei, "The Coming Crisis of China's
One-Party Regime," *Project Syndicate*, September 20, 2019, http://project-syndicate
.org/commentary/crisis-of-chinese-communist-party-by-minxin-pei-2019-09; Shyam
Saran, "China's Cup of Troubles," *Tribune*, August 13, 2019, http://tribuneindia.com
/news/comment/china-s-cup-of-troubles/817202.html; Bret Stephens, "Is China
Heading for Crisis?," *New York Times*, October 3, 2019, http://nytimes.com/2019/10
/03/opinion/china-xi-jinping.html; Stratfor, "A Decisive Moment for China Draws
Nigh," August 22, 2019, http://worldview.stratfor.com/article/decisive-moment-china
-nigh-beidaihe-political-meeting; Stratfor, "The Geopolitics of China: A Great Power
Enclosed," March 25, 2012, http://worldview.stratfor.com/article/geopolitics-china
-great-power-enclosed; and Nathaniel Taplin, "China's Inward Tilt Could Cripple It,"
Wall Street Journal, June 26, 2019, http://wsj.com/articles/chinas-inward-tilt-could
-cripple-it-11561543149.

33. This rigorous definition of U.S. national interests has been developed over twenty-five
years in an enduring conversation and partnership with Graham Allison. See Graham
Allison and Robert Blackwill, *America's National Interests* (Commission on America's
National Interests, 2000), http://belfercenter.org/files/amernatinter.pdf.

34. See also Robert D. Blackwill, "Defending U.S. Vital Interests: Prescriptions for Trump,"
Foreign Policy, January 25, 2017, http://foreignpolicy.com/2017/01/25/defending
-vital-u-s-interests-policy-prescriptions-for-trump.

35. President Trump makes a mockery of all these elements of successful U.S. foreign policy.

36. Odd Arne Westad, "The Sources of Chinese Conduct," *Foreign Affairs*, September/
October 2019, http://foreignaffairs.com/articles/china/2019-08-12/sources
-chinese-conduct.

37. Xi Jinping, "New Asian Security Concept for New Progress in Security Cooperation,"
remarks at the Fourth Summit of the Conference on Interaction and Confidence
Building Measures in Asia, Shanghai, May 21, 2014. The fact that Beijing has not

repeated this concept because of its immediate blowback does not diminish its centrality to the thinking of China's leadership.

38. Much of this chapter is reprinted with permission from Blackwill and Tellis, *Revising U.S. Grand Strategy Toward China.*

39. Richard K. Betts and Walter A. McDougall think not, because they believe that no nation can successfully formulate and implement a grand strategy. See Richard K. Betts, "Is Strategy an Illusion?" *International Security* 25, no. 2 (Fall 2000): 5–50; and Walter A. McDougall, "Can the United States Do Grand Strategy?" *Orbis* 54, no. 2 (2010): 165–184, http://doi.org/10.1016/j.orbis.2010.01.008. See also Yan Xuetong, "The Age of Uneasy Peace: Chinese Power in a Divided World," *Foreign Affairs,* January/February 2019, http://foreignaffairs.com/articles/china/2018-12-11/age -uneasy-peace. Others argue that there is something unique about China that hinders grand strategy; they stress how difficult centralized policy is in China, which is what Xi is trying to change. See Angela Stanzel, Nadege Rolland, Jabin Jacob, and Melanie Hart, "Does China Have a 'Grand Strategy'?" European Council on Foreign Relations, October 18, 2017, http://ecfr.eu/publications/summary/grands_designs_does_china _have_a_grand_strategy. Given the many relevant statements by the Chinese government, I am unconvinced by both these arguments.

40. The Chinese government, of course, does not admit that these are all part of China's grand strategy. See Jie Sheng Li, "A Primer on China's New White Paper," *Diplomatic Courier,* October 17, 2019, http://diplomaticourier.com/posts/a-primer-on-chinas -new-white-paper.

41. Henry Kissinger, *A World Restored: Metternich, Castlereagh and the Problems of Peace, 1812–1822* (London: Phoenix Press, 2000), 2–3.

42. See Doug Bandow, "China Isn't an Enemy and Hawks Shouldn't Turn It Into One," *American Conservative,* May 9, 2019, http://theamericanconservative.com/articles /china-isnt-an-enemy-and-hawks-shouldnt-turn-it-into-one; Editorial Board, "The U.S. and China Don't Need to Be Enemies," Bloomberg, July 1, 2019, http:// bloomberg.com/opinion/articles/2019-07-01/trump-xi-truce-at-g-20-should-lead -to-broader-u-s-china-deal; and Kishore Mahbubani, "What China Threat?," *Harper's Magazine,* February 2019, http://harpers.org/archive/2019/02/what-china-threat.

43. The argument by Charles Edel and Hal Brands that this is a struggle with strong parallels to the Cold War is unconvincing. To apply the rigorous methodology of the late great diplomatic historian Ernest May, it is different in too many fundamental ways. Charles Edel and Hal Brands, "The Real Origins of the U.S.-China Cold War," *Foreign Policy,* June 2, 2019, http://foreignpolicy.com/2019/06/02/the-real-origins-of -the-u-s-china-cold-war-big-think-communism.

44. James Massola, "Barack Obama's China Policy Has Not Been Successful, Says US Official," *Sydney Morning Herald,* November 2, 2014, http://smh.com.au/politics /federal/barack-obamas-china-policy-has-not-been-successful-says-us-official- 20141101-11e461.html.

45. For China's integration into the international system, see Beckley, "Stop Obsessing About China"; and Michael J. Mazarr, Timothy R. Heath, and Astrid Stuth Cevallos, *China and the International Order* (Santa Monica, CA: RAND Corporation, 2018), http://rand.org/pubs/research_reports/RR2423.html.

46. See Ellen Ioanes, "Navy SEAL Who Oversaw the bin Laden Raid Says China's Massive Military Buildup Is a 'Holy S---' Moment," *Business Insider*, September 18, 2019, http://businessinsider.com/seal-mcraven-chinas-military-buildup-moment-for-us-2019-9; and "Pentagon Policy Chief Singles Out China as Biggest Threat to the U.S.," NorthcentralPA.com, September 24, 2019, http://northcentralpa.com/news/international/pentagon-policy-chief-singles-out-china-as-biggest-threat-to/article_b4c086c5-c97f-517b-99b6-098927703cd0.html.

47. Donald Trump has intensified all these allied concerns and is likely to continue to do so as long as he is president.

48. See Chas W. Freeman, "The Sino-American Split and Its Consequences" (lecture, Foreign Policy Association Centennial Lecture Series, New York, June 13, 2019), http://chasfreeman.net/the-sino-american-split-and-its-consequences; and Nahal Toosi, "'When Paradigms Die': China Veterans Fear Extinction in Trump's Washington," *Politico*, July 28, 2019, http://politico.com/story/2019/07/28/trump-china-veterans-foreign-policy-1438389.

49. M. Taylor Fravel et al., "China Is Not an Enemy," *Washington Post*, July 3, 2019, http://washingtonpost.com/opinions/making-china-a-us-enemy-is-counterproductive/2019/07/02/647d49d0-9bfa-11e9-b27f-ed2942f73d70_story.html.

50. Following the *Washington Post* letter, a counter text was published. See James E. Fanell, "Stay the Course on China: An Open Letter to President Trump," *Journal of Political Risk*, July 18, 2019, http://jpolrisk.com/stay-the-course-on-china-an-open-letter-to-president-trump. For an analysis of perceived shortcomings on both sides of this rift, see Howard W. French, "What America's China Debate Gets Right and Wrong—and What It's Missing," *World Politics Review*, July 31, 2019, http://worldpoliticsreview.com/articles/28082/what-america-s-china-debate-gets-right-and-wrong-and-what-it-s-missing.

51. On August 23, 2019, Trump tweeted: ". . . My only question is, who is our bigger enemy, Jay Powell or Chairman Xi?" but one tweet hardly negates the general point being made here, especially since he included as an enemy the chairman of the Federal Reserve Bank. See Donald J. Trump (@realDonaldTrump), Twitter, August 23, 2019, 10:57 a.m., http://twitter.com/realDonaldTrump/status/1164914610836783104.

52. See Daniel R. Russel and Blake Berger, "Navigating the Belt and Road Initiative," Asia Society Policy Institute, June 2019, http://asiasociety.org/sites/default/files/2019-06/Navigating the Belt and Road Initiative_2.pdf; Lily Kuo, "'Divide and Conquer': China Puts the Pressure on U.S. Allies," *Guardian*, February 2, 2019, http://theguardian.com/world/2019/feb/02/divide-and-conquer-china-puts-the-pressure-on-us-allies; Blackwill and Harris, *War by Other Means,* 93–151; Blackwill, "Indo-Pacific Strategy in an Era of Geoeconomics"; Doug Palmer and Ben White, "Treasury Designates China as a Currency Manipulator," *Politico*, August 5, 2019, http://politico.com/story/2019/08/05/trump-blasts-china-yuan-drop-as-currency-manipulation-1634502; Blackwill and Tellis, *Revising U.S. Grand Strategy Toward China*; The Commission on the Theft of American Intellectual Property, *Update to the IP Commission Report: The Theft of American Intellectual Property; Reassessments of the Challenge and United States Policy* (Washington, DC: National Bureau of Asian Research, 2017), http://ipcommission.org/report/IP_Commission_Report_Update_2017.pdf; Gerry Shih, "Xi Offers Promises and Threats as He Calls China's Unification With Taiwan Inevitable,"

Washington Post, January 2, 2019, http://washingtonpost.com/world/asia_pacific/xi
-offers-promises-and-threats-as-he-calls-chinas-unification-with-taiwan-inevitable
/2019/01/02/85ae5ece-0e82-11e9-92b8-6dd99e2d80e1_story.html; U.S. Senate
Committee on Armed Services, "Advance Policy Questions for Admiral Philip
Davidson, USN, Expected Nominee for Commander, U.S. Pacific Command," April
17, 2018, http://armed-services.senate.gov/imo/media/doc/Davidson_APQs_04-17
-18.pdf; Blackwill and Campbell, *Xi Jinping on the Global Stage*; U.S. Library of
Congress, Congressional Research Service, *U.S.-China Strategic Competition in South
and East China Seas: Background and Issues for Congress,* by Ronald O'Rourke, R42784
(2019), http://assets.documentcloud.org/documents/6432463/U-S-China-Strategic
-Competition-in-South-and.pdf; Human Rights Watch, "China," in *World Report
2019,* http://hrw.org/world-report/2019/country-chapters/china-and-tibet; and Anne
Applebaum, "'Never Again?' It's Already Happening," *Washington Post*, February 15,
2019, http://washingtonpost.com/opinions/global-opinions/the-west-ignored-crimes
-against-humanity-in-the-1930s-its-happening-again-now/2019/02/15/d17d4998-
3130-11e9-813a-0ab2f17e305b_story.html.

53. For a concise assertion of the consequences of an inadequate response to Chinese
power, see Joseph W. Sullivan, "Every American Should Hope Trump Prevails Against
China," *Atlantic*, August 20, 2019, http://theatlantic.com/ideas/archive/2019/08/china
-vs-democracy/596248.

54. See Blackwill, *Trump's Foreign Policies Are Better Than They Seem.*

55. For Trump's poisonous effects on U.S. domestic institutions and societal cohesion,
see Blackwill, *Trump's Foreign Policies Are Better Than They Seem*; Hannah Fingerhut,
"Polls Show Sour Views of Race Relations in Trump's America," Associated Press, July
16, 2019, http://apnews.com/277fe31ea2234658a991243a9c6f2466; and Stephen
M. Walt, "America Can't Be Trusted Anymore," *Foreign Policy*, April 10, 2018, http://
foreignpolicy.com/2018/04/10/america-cant-be-trusted-anymore.

56. Some wonder if Democrats are capable of carrying out ambitious policy prescriptions
such as those in this report. One can only hope that these worries will not be realized.
See Peter Beinart, "But What About China?" *Atlantic*, August 1, 2019, http://theatlantic
.com/ideas/archive/2019/08/debates-democrats-sounded-if-china-doesnt-exist/595273;
David Ignatius, "Democrats Need to Stop Running Scared on Foreign Policy,"
Washington Post, August 13, 2019, http://washingtonpost.com/opinions/global-opinions
/democrats-need-to-stop-running-scared-on-foreign-policy/2019/08/13/92c525c2
-bde4-11e9-9b73-fd3c65ef8f9c_story.html; and Michael Schuman, "The Discord of the
U.S. Stance Against China," *Atlantic*, July 29, 2019, http://theatlantic.com/international
/archive/2019/07/how-will-democrats-deal-china/594817.

57. See Richard N. Haass's encompassing *Foreign Policy Begins at Home: The Case for
Putting America's House in Order* (New York: Basic Books, 2013) for a "to do" agenda
to reenergize the United States. For a diagnosis of some of the domestic issues facing
the United States, see Lawrence H. Summers, "We No Longer Share a Common Lived
Experience," *Washington Post*, October 9, 2019, http://washingtonpost.com/opinions
/we-no-longer-share-a-common-lived-experience/2019/10/08/f037b9e4-e9eb-11e9
-9c6d-436a0df4f31d_story.html.

58. For cautiously optimistic views of the U.S. ability to reinvent itself yet again, see James
Fallows, "The Reinvention of America," *Atlantic*, May 2018, http://theatlantic.com

/magazine/archive/2018/05/reinventing-america/556856; Walter Russell Mead, "The Big Shift," *Foreign Affairs*, May/June 2019, http://foreignaffairs.com/articles/united -states/2018-04-16/big-shift; and Ali Wyne, "How the US Should Frame Its Approach to China," *Financial Times*, July 24, 2019, http://ft.com/content/851931ea-adfc-11e9 -8030-530adfa879c2.

59. For just a few of the president's many damaging tweets on this subject, see Donald J. Trump (@realDonaldTrump), "Justice Roberts can say what he wants, but the 9th Circuit is a complete & total disaster. It is out of control, has a horrible reputation, is overturned more than any Circuit in the Country, 79%, & is used to get an almost guaranteed result. Judges must not Legislate Security . . . ," Twitter, November 22, 2018, 4:21 a.m., http://twitter.com/realdonaldtrump/status/1065581119242940416; Donald J. Trump (@realDonaldTrump), "As usual, Powell let us down, but at least he is ending quantitative tightening, which shouldn't have started in the first place - no inflation. We are winning anyway, but I am certainly not getting much help from the Federal Reserve!," Twitter, July 31, 2019, 1:41p.m., http://twitter.com/realdonaldtrump/status /1156666164732473345; Donald J. Trump (@realDonaldTrump), "58,000 non-citizens voted in Texas, with 95,000 non-citizens registered to vote. These numbers are just the tip of the iceberg. All over the country, especially in California, voter fraud is rampant. Must be stopped. Strong voter ID! @foxandfriends," Twitter, January 27, 2019, 5:22 a.m., http://twitter.com/realdonaldtrump/status/1089513936435716096; and Donald J. Trump (@realDonaldTrump), "Look how things have turned around on the Criminal Deep State. They go after Phony Collusion with Russia, a made up Scam, and end up getting caught in a major SPY scandal the likes of which this country may never have seen before! What goes around, comes around!," Twitter, May 23, 2018, 3:54 a.m., http://twitter.com/realdonaldtrump/status/999242039723163648.

60. See *Statement Before the National Commission on Military, National, and Public Service* (2019) (written statement by Suzanne Spaulding and Elizabeth Rindskopf Parker on behalf of the Defending Democratic Institutions Project at the Center for Strategic and International Studies), http://csis-prod.s3.amazonaws.com/s3fs-public /publication/190710_spaulding_testimony.pdf.

61. Annenberg Public Policy Center, "Americans' Knowledge of the Branches of Government Is Declining," September 13, 2016, http://annenbergpublicpolicycenter .org/americans-knowledge-of-the-branches-of-government-is-declining.

62. Jonathan Gould, ed., *Guardian of Democracy: The Civic Mission of Schools, Center for Information and Research on Civic Learning and Engagement* (New York: Carnegie Corporation of New York, 2011), 6, http://carnegie.org/media/filer_public/ab/dd /abdda62e-6e84-47a4-a043-348d2f2085ae/ccny_grantee_2011_guardian.pdf.

63. See Anne Applebaum, "Americans Spent Decades Discussing Rule of Law. Why Would Anyone Believe Us Now?," *Washington Post*, September 27, 2019, http:// washingtonpost.com/opinions/global-opinions/americans-spent-decades-discussing -rule-of-law-why-would-anyone-believe-us-now/2019/09/27/a02d9c36-e142-11e9 -8dc8-498eabc129a0_story.html; Tarun Chhabra, Rush Doshi, Ryan Hass, and Mira Rapp-Hooper, "Rethinking US-China Competition: Next Generation Perspectives," interview by Bruce Jones, ed. Bruce Jones and Will Moreland, Brookings Institution, June 2019, http://brookings.edu/wp-content/uploads/2019/06/FP_20190625_global _china.pdf; Michael Gerson, "Trump Is Turning American Ideology Into a Sham," *Washington Post*, October 17, 2019, http://washingtonpost.com/opinions/trump-is

-turning-american-ideology-into-a-sham/2019/10/17/fcae91fa-f118-11e9-8693
-f487e46784aa_story.html; and Ishaan Tharoor, "Trump's Impeachment Battle Is Part
of a Bigger Global Crisis in Democracy," *Washington Post*, October 4, 2019, http://
washingtonpost.com/world/2019/10/04/trumps-impeachment-battle-is-part-bigger
-global-crisis-democracy.

64. John F. Kennedy, first presidential debate with Richard M. Nixon, CBS Studios,
Chicago, September 26, 1960, http://jfklibrary.org/archives/other-resources/john
-f-kennedy-speeches/1st-nixon-kennedy-debate-19600926.

65. The Trump administration (but not always the president) fails on this final
collaborative point, instead almost entirely emphasizing the competitive components
of the bilateral relationship. Nevertheless, the U.S. public apparently is not convinced.
In a February 2019 poll conducted by the Chicago Council on Global Affairs, two-
thirds of Americans (68 percent) say the United States should pursue a policy of
friendly cooperation and engagement with China; one-third (31 percent) advocates
working to limit the growth of China's power. This needs to change. Craig Kafura,
"Public Prefers Cooperation and Engagement With China," Chicago Council on
Global Affairs, October 9, 2019, http://thechicagocouncil.org/publication/public
-prefers-cooperation-and-engagement-china.

66. For a similar viewpoint, see *Strategic Competition With China, Before the H. Comm
on Armed Services*, 115th Cong. (4–5) (2018) (statement by Ely Ratner, Council
on Foreign Relations), http://cfr.org/sites/default/files/report_pdf/Strategic%20
Competition%20with%20China%20HASC%202%2015%2018.pdf.

67. *Strategic Competition With China, Before the H. Comm on Armed Services*, 5.

68. See *Strategic Competition With China, Before the H. Comm on Armed Services*, 5.

69. See *Hearing on China's Belt and Road Initiative, Before the Senate Finance Comm.
Subcom. on International Trade, Customs, and Global Competitiveness,* 116th Cong.
(6) (2019) (statement by Daniel Kliman, Center for a New American Security), http://
s3.amazonaws.com/files.cnas.org/documents/Daniel-Kliman_Testimony-for-Senate
-Finance-Committee-Trade-Subcommittee_FINAL-min.pdf?mtime=20190617115736.

70. See *Strategic Competition With China, Before the H. Comm on Armed Services*, 7.

71. Prescriptions in this paragraph take direction from *Strategic Competition With China,
Before the H. Comm on Armed Services*, 6.

72. Eduardo Porter and Karl Russell, "Firing Back at Trump in the Trade War With Tariffs
Aimed at His Base," *New York Times,* October 3, 2018, http://nytimes.com/interactive
/2018/10/03/business/economy/china-tariff-retaliation.html.

73. Porter and Russell, "Firing Back at Trump in the Trade War With Tariffs Aimed at
His Base."

74. These policy prescriptions may seem naive given the current vicious partisan
atmosphere in Washington. Yet they are based on the constitutional responsibilities
of the president and Congress. The White House and the Hill need to act together
to protect the country. See Henry Olsen, "Trump Is Standing Firm Against
China. Congress Must Stand With Him," *Washington Post*, May 6, 2019, http://
washingtonpost.com/opinions/2019/05/06/trump-is-standing-firm-against-china
-congress-must-stand-with-him.

75. Brian Spegele and Kate O'Keeffe, "China Maneuvers to Snag Top-Secret Boeing Satellite Technology," *Wall Street Journal*, December 4, 2018, http://wsj.com/articles /china-maneuvers-to-snag-top-secret-boeing-satellite-technology-1543943490.

76. Lingling Wei and Bob Davis, "How China Systematically Pries Technology From U.S. Companies," *Wall Street Journal*, September 26, 2018, http://wsj.com/articles/how -china-systematically-pries-technology-from-u-s-companies-1537972066.

77. Ana Swanson, "Trump Officials Battle Over Plan to Keep Technology Out of Chinese Hands," *New York Times*, October 23, 2019, http://nytimes.com/2019/10/23/business /trump-technology-china-trade.html.

78. For a similar position, see Melanie Hart and Kelly Magsamen, "Limit, Leverage, and Compete: A New Strategy on China," Center for American Progress, April 2019, 17, http://americanprogress.org/issues/security/reports/2019/04/03/468136/limit -leverage-compete-new-strategy-china.

79. See Lee G. Branstetter, "China's Forced Technology Transfer Problem—and What to Do About It," Peterson Institute of International Economics, June 2018, 8, http://piie .com/system/files/documents/pb18-13.pdf.

80. See Branstetter, "China's Forced Technology Transfer Problem—and What to Do About It," 7, 8.

81. Special thanks to CFR colleague Adam Segal for his thoughtful comments on U.S. AI policy. For details on the National Security Commission on Artificial Intelligence, see Robert Work and Eric Schmidt, "In Search of Ideas: The National Security Commission on Artificial Intelligence Wants You," *War on the Rocks*, July 18, 2019, http://warontherocks.com/2019/07/in-search-of-ideas-the-national-security -commission-on-artificial-intelligence-wants-you. Also see Kaveh Waddell, "The Global Race Between China and U.S. to Set the Rules for AI," Axios, July 14, 2019, http://axios.com/artificial-intelligence-china-united-states-5bea5020-c5c6-4527 -8d25-7bf0036f6384.html. AI is not the only dual-use area that has seen significant Chinese research investment. See Jeanne Whalen, "The Quantum Revolution Is Coming, and Chinese Scientists Are at the Forefront," *Washington Post*, August 18, 2019, http://washingtonpost.com/business/2019/08/18/quantum-revolution-is -coming-chinese-scientists-are-forefront. For an example of U.S. efforts in this domain, see Cade Metz, "Google Claims a Quantum Breakthrough That Could Change Computing," *New York Times*, October 23, 2019, http://nytimes.com/2019/10 /23/technology/quantum-computing-google.html.

82. See Eric Lofgren, "A Guide to Not Killing or Mutilating Artificial Intelligence Research," *War on the Rocks*, August 16, 2019, http://warontherocks.com/2019/08/a -guide-to-not-killing-or-mutilating-artificial-intelligence-research; and Paul Scharre, "How Congress Can Help Ensure US Leadership in Artificial Intelligence," *Hill*, January 16, 2019, http://thehill.com/opinion/technology/425309-how-congress-can -help-ensure-us-leadership-in-artificial-intelligence.

83. U.S. Senator Martin Heinrich of New Mexico, "Heinrich, Portman, Schatz Propose National Strategy for Artificial Intelligence; Call for $2.2 Billion Investment in Education, Research & Development," May 21, 2019, http://heinrich.senate.gov/press -releases/heinrich-portman-schatz-propose-national-strategy-for-artificial-intelligence -call-for-22-billion-investment-in-education-research-and-development; and Reuters,

"Beijing to Build $2 Billion AI Research Park: Xinhua," January 3, 2018, http://reuters
.com/article/us-china-artificial-intelligence/beijing-to-build-2-billion-ai-research-park
-xinhua-idUSKBN1ES0B8.

84. See Council on Foreign Relations, *Innovation and National Security: Keeping Our Edge*
(New York: Council on Foreign Relations, 2019), 54–59.

85. For ideas on how to fund U.S. AI initiatives, see William A. Carter, Emma Kinnucan,
and Josh Elliot, "A National Machine Intelligence Strategy for the United States,"
Center for Strategic and International Studies and Booz Allen Hamilton, March 2018,
21, http://csis-prod.s3.amazonaws.com/s3fs-public/publication/180227_Carter
_MachineIntelligence_Web.PDF; and Scharre, "How Congress Can Help Ensure US
Leadership in Artificial Intelligence." For a compelling argument about the importance
of AI safety, see Danielle C. Tarraf, "Our Future Lies in Making AI Robust and
Verifiable," *War on the Rocks*, October 22, 2019, http://warontherocks.com/2019/10
/our-future-lies-in-making-ai-robust-and-verifiable.

86. Ana Swanson, Paul Mozur, and Steve Lohr, "U.S. Blacklists More Chinese Tech
Companies Over National Security Concerns," *New York Times*, June 21, 2019, http://
nytimes.com/2019/06/21/us/politics/us-china-trade-blacklist.html. See Council on
Foreign Relations, *Innovation and National Security*, 46–52.

87. See Carter, Kinnucan, and Elliot, "A National Machine Intelligence Strategy," 36–37;
and Organisation for Economic Co-operation and Development, "Recommendation
of the Council on Artificial Intelligence," § IV.2.3, http://legalinstruments.oecd.org
/en/instruments/OECD-LEGAL-0449.

88. Kai-Fu Lee and Paul Triolo, "China's Artificial Intelligence Revolution: Understanding
Beijing's Structural Advantages," Eurasia Group, December 2017, http://eurasiagroup
.net/files/upload/China_Embraces_AI.pdf.

89. For views on the detrimental effects of poor private-public AI cooperation, see Peter
Thiel, "Good for Google, Bad for America," *New York Times*, August 1, 2019, http://
nytimes.com/2019/08/01/opinion/peter-thiel-google.html; and Tom Upchurch, "How
China Could Beat the West in the Deadly Race for AI Weapons," *Wired*, August 8,
2018, http://wired.co.uk/article/artificial-intelligence-weapons-warfare-project-maven
-google-china. See also Don Clark, "Pentagon, With an Eye on China, Pushes for Help
From American Tech," *New York Times*, October 25, 2019, http://nytimes.com/2019
/10/25/technology/pentagon-taiwan-tsmc-chipmaker.html; and Eric Rosenbach and
Katherine Mansted, "How to Win the Battle Over Data," Belfer Center for Science and
International Affairs, September 17, 2019, http://belfercenter.org/publication/how
-win-battle-over-data.

90. Ryan Pickrell, "The Pentagon Admitted It Will Lose to China on AI If It Doesn't Make
Some Big Changes," *Business Insider*, August 30, 2019, http://businessinsider.com
/pentagon-admits-china-could-outpace-us-on-ai-without-changes-2019-8.

91. Eric Schmidt, former head of Google, vividly makes the point: "The policy of America to
deny visas to technically trained people in the U.S. and shipped to other countries, where
they create companies that compete with America, has to be the stupidest policy of all
the U.S. government policies." Julia Boorstin, "Eric Schmidt Talks Motorola, Microsoft
Immigration and NSA," CNBC, July 12, 2013, http://cnbc.com/id/100882325.

92. See Council on Foreign Relations, *Innovation and National Security*, 60–61.

93. See Council on Foreign Relations, *Innovation and National Security*, 62.

94. The United States should aggressively seek leadership positions and influence in international standard-setting bodies. The Trump administration has withdrawn from just such organizations.

95. See Carter, Kinnucan, and Elliot, "A National Machine Intelligence Strategy," 40, 45; and Waddell, "The Global Race Between China and U.S. to Set the Rules for AI."

96. See Peter Cihon, "Standards for AI Governance: International Standards to Enable Global Coordination in AI Research and Development," Future of Humanity Institute, University of Oxford, April 2019, http://www.fhi.ox.ac.uk/wp-content/uploads /Standards_-FHI-Technical-Report.pdf.

97. See Waddell, "The Global Race Between China and U.S. to Set the Rules for AI."

98. As Henry Kissinger has put it, "No country can act wisely simultaneously in every part of the globe at every moment of time." Henry A. Kissinger, "Central Issues of American Foreign Policy," in *Agenda for the Nation*, ed. Kermit Gordon (Washington, DC: Brookings Institution, 1968), 599. Secretary Pompeo in theory appears to understand the concept. But nevertheless, many of the administration's policies do not operationally reflect it. See Associated Press, "'First Thing I Do Is Read About China,' Mike Pompeo Says on US Foreign Policy Priorities," *South China Morning Post*, July 30, 2019, http://scmp.com/news/china/article/3020562/first-thing-i-do-read -about-china-mike-pompeo-says-us-foreign-policy. See also Mackenzie Eaglen, "Just Say No: The Pentagon Needs to Drop the Distractions and Move Great Power Competition Beyond Lip Service," *War on the Rocks*, October 28, 2019, http:// warontherocks.com/2019/10/just-say-no-the-pentagon-needs-to-drop-the-distractions -and-move-great-power-competition-beyond-lip-service.

99. See Patricia M. Kim, "China's Quest for Influence in Northeast Asia," in *China's Expanding Strategic Ambitions*, eds. Ashley J. Tellis, Alison Szalwinski, and Michael Wills (Seattle: The National Bureau of Asian Research, 2019); Oriana Skylar Mastro, "Dynamic Dilemmas: China's Evolving Northeast Asia Security Strategy," *Joint U.S. -Korea Academic Studies* 27 (2016): 9–23, http://fpri.org/wp-content/uploads/2016/12 /final_kei_jointus-korea_2016_161010.pdf; and Laura Zhou and Lee Jeong-ho, "China Set to Strengthen Economic Ties With Japan, South Korea Amid Trade Row With United States," *South China Morning Post*, May 8, 2018, http://scmp.com/news/china/diplomacy -defence/article/2145215/china-set-strengthen-economic-ties-japan-south-korea.

100. See *Hearing on China's Growing Influence in Asia and the United States, Before the Subcomm. on Asia, the Pacific, and Nonproliferation*, 116th Cong. (2019) (statement of Daniel Kliman of the Center for a New American Security), http://s3.amazonaws.com /files.cnas.org/documents/Daniel-Kliman_Final-Testimony-for-HFAC-Subcommittee -on-Asia-the-Pacific-and-Nonproliferation-min.pdf?mtime=20190508124206; Joshua Kurlantzick, "China's Soft and Sharp Power Strategies in Southeast Asia Accelerating, but Are They Having an Impact?," Council on Foreign Relations, July 29, 2019, http:// cfr.org/blog/chinas-soft-and-sharp-power-strategies-southeast-asia-accelerating-are -they-having-impact; and Bernhard Zand, "Operation Mekong: China Solidifies Its Influence in Southeast Asia," *Spiegel Online*, October 11, 2018, http://spiegel.de /international/world/operation-mekong-china-tightens-grip-on-southeast-asia-a -1232484.html.

101. See Rubeena Mahato, "India and the West Are Concerned About China's Growing Influence in South Asia—South Asians Should Be, Too," *South China Morning Post*, October 18, 2018, http://scmp.com/comment/insight-opinion/asia/article/2169108 /india-and-west-are-concerned-about-chinas-growing; Kevin Rudd, "Growing Chinese Influence in South Asia," interview by Jyoti Malhotra, *The Print*, October 1, 2018, http://asiasociety.org/policy-institute/growing-chinese-influence-south-asia; and Hampton Stephens, "The India-China Rivalry Heats Up in South Asia," *World Politics Review*, March 27, 2019, http://worldpoliticsreview.com/insights/25400/the-india -china-rivalry-heats-up-in-south-asia.

102. See Nike Ching, "Kiribati Cuts Diplomatic Ties to Taiwan in Favor of China," Voice of America, September 20, 2019, http://voanews.com/east-asia-pacific/kiribati-cuts -diplomatic-ties-taiwan-favor-china; David Crawshaw and Gerry Shih, "China Intensifies Pacific Offensive as Taiwan Loses Another Ally," *Washington Post*, September 20, 2019, http://washingtonpost.com/world/asia_pacific/chinas-pacific -offensive-intensifies-as-taiwan-cuts-relations-with-kiribati/2019/09/20/bccd26d8- db69-11e9-a1a5-162b8a9c9ca2_story.html; Kathrin Hille, "Pacific Islands: A New Arena of Rivalry Between China and the US," *Financial Times*, April 8, 2019, http:// ft.com/content/bdbb8ada-59dc-11e9-939a-341f5ada9d40; Julia Hollingsworth, "Why China Is Challenging Australia for Influence Over the Pacific Islands," CNN, July 22, 2019, http://cnn.com/2019/07/22/asia/china-australia-pacific-investment-intl-hnk /index.html; and Laura Zhou, "China's Growing Role in South Pacific Nations Cannot Be Stopped, Says Vice-Minister Zheng Zeguang," *South China Morning Post*, November 13, 2018, http://scmp.com/news/china/diplomacy/article/2173025/chinas -growing-role-south-pacific-nations-cannot-be-stopped.

103. See Kemal Kirisci and Philippe Le Corre, "The New Geopolitics of Central Asia: China Vies for Influence in Russia's Backyard," Brookings Institution, January 2, 2018, http:// brookings.edu/blog/order-from-chaos/2018/01/02/the-new-geopolitics-of-central-asia -china-vies-for-influence-in-russias-backyard; Martha Brill Olcott, "China's Unmatched Influence in Central Asia," Carnegie Endowment for International Peace, September 18, 2013, http://carnegieendowment.org/2013/09/18/china-s-unmatched-influence-in -central-asia-pub-53035; and Gerry Shih, "In Central Asia's Forbidding Highlands, a Quiet Newcomer: Chinese Troops," *Washington Post*, February 18, 2019, http:// washingtonpost.com/world/asia_pacific/in-central-asias-forbidding-highlands-a-quiet -newcomer-chinese-troops/2019/02/18/78d4a8d0-1e62-11e9-a759-2b8541bbbe20_ story.html.

104. See Daniel Kliman and Abigail Grace, "China Smells Opportunity in the Middle East's Crisis," *Foreign Policy*, June 14, 2018, http://foreignpolicy.com/2018/06/14 /china-smells-opportunity-in-the-middle-easts-crisis; Stratfor, "China May Set Its Navy on Course for the Persian Gulf," August 9, 2019, http://worldview.stratfor.com /article/china-naval-operations-persian-gulf-maritime-escort; Daniel Wagner, "China Rewrites the Rules on How to Rise in Influence in the Middle East," *South China Morning Post*, January 31, 2018, http://scmp.com/comment/insight-opinion/article /2131328/china-rewrites-rules-how-rise-influence-middle-east; and Aime Williams, "Pentagon Warns of China's Growing Influence in the Middle East," *Financial Times*, August 21, 2019, http://ft.com/content/4a9b008a-c2be-11e9-a8e9-296ca66511c9.

105. See Tomi Huhtanen, "Is Russia Sleepwalking Into Chinese Dominance?," Wilfried Martens Centre for European Studies, April 15, 2019, http://martenscentre.eu/blog

/russia-sleepwalking-chinese-dominance; "Chinese Invest in New Gas Project in Russian Far East," *Moscow Times*, September 4, 2019, http://themoscowtimes.com/2019 /09/04/chinese-invest-in-new-gas-project-in-russian-far-east-a67135; and Eric Ng, "China's Russian Buying Spree to Continue, Says Leading Moscow Investment Bank," *South China Morning Post*, November 19, 2017, http://scmp.com/business/companies /article/2120571/chinas-russian-buying-spree-continue-says-leading-moscow.

106. See Peter Martin and Alan Crawford, "China's Influence Digs Deep Into Europe's Political Landscape," Bloomberg, April 3, 2019, http://bloomberg.com/news/articles /2019-04-03/china-s-influence-digs-deep-into-europe-s-political-landscape; Dusan Stojanovic, "China's Spreading Influence in Eastern Europe Worries West," Associated Press, April 10, 2019, http://apnews.com/d121bfc580f04e73b886cc8c5a155f7e; and Valbona Zeneli, "Mapping China's Investments in Europe," *Diplomat*, March 14, 2019, http://thediplomat.com/2019/03/mapping-chinas-investments-in-europe.

107. See Krishnadev Calamur, "Tillerson to Latin America: Beware of China," *Atlantic*, February 3, 2018, http://theatlantic.com/international/archive/2018/02/rex-in-latam /552197; Ulises Granados, "Gauging China's Military Intentions in Latin America," WorldCrunch, September 13, 2019, http://worldcrunch.com/opinion-analysis/gauging -china39s-military-intentions-in-latin-america; Ernesto Londono, "To Influence El Salvador, China Dangled Money. The U.S. Made Threats," *New York Times*, September 21, 2019, http://nytimes.com/2019/09/21/world/americas/china-el -salvador-trump-backlash.html; Carlos Roa, "The United States Is Losing Latin America to China," *National Interest*, August 15, 2019, http://nationalinterest.org /feature/united-states-losing-latin-america-china-73906; and Carlos Gustavo Poggio Teixeira and Fernanda Magnotta, "Americas for the Chinese? US Should Tend to Its Own 'Backyard,'" *Hill*, November 20, 2018, http://thehill.com/opinion/national -security/417502-americas-for-the-chinese-us-should-tend-to-its-own-backyard.

108. See Eleanor Albert, "China in Africa," Council on Foreign Relations, July 12, 2017, http://cfr.org/backgrounder/china-africa; Aubrey Hruby, "In Africa, China Is the News," *Foreign Policy*, August 13, 2019, http://foreignpolicy.com/2019/08/13/in-africa -china-is-the-news; and Nick Turse, "U.S. Generals Worry About Russian and Chinese Influence in Africa, Documents Show," *Intercept*, August 13, 2019, http://theintercept .com/2019/08/13/russia-china-military-africa.

109. See David Auerswald, "China's Multifaceted Arctic Strategy," *War on the Rocks*, May 24, 2019, http://warontherocks.com/2019/05/chinas-multifaceted-arctic-strategy; Bethlehem Feleke, "With an Eye to Power and Profit, Beijing Is Building Influence in the Arctic," CNN, December 30, 2018, http://cnn.com/2018/12/29/asia/china-arctic -influence-intl/index.html; and Somini Sengupta and Steven Lee Myers, "Latest Arena for China's Growing Global Ambitions: The Arctic," *New York Times*, May 24, 2019, http://nytimes.com/2019/05/24/climate/china-arctic.html.

110. President Trump's October 2019 decision—through late-night tweet thread—to withdraw all U.S. troops from Syria, and then his poisonous explanation of it, is just one of many examples. See Donald J. Trump (@realDonaldTrump), "As I have stated strongly before, and just to reiterate, if Turkey does anything that I, in my great and unmatched wisdom, consider to be off limits, I will totally destroy and obliterate the Economy of Turkey (I've done before!)," Twitter, October 7, 2019, 11:38 a.m., http:// twitter.com/realDonaldTrump/status/1181232249821388801.

111. I do not have in mind Donald Trump's feckless infatuation with Vladimir Putin and his policies.

112. Every American president since 1945 until Donald Trump understood that democratic values are a crucial component of the U.S. alliance systems. Henry Kissinger stresses, "Similarly, our allies' confidence that peace was the goal of our foreign policy was the prerequisite of the cohesion of our alliances. We could resist aggressive policies best from a platform of peace; men and women of goodwill and decency could be enlisted only in support of a policy of positive aspirations. But the responsibility of leaders is not simply to affirm an objective. It is above all to endow it with a meaning compatible with the values of their society." Kissinger, *Years of Upheaval*, 979. Also see Ash Carter, "Reflections on American Grand Strategy in Asia," Belfer Center for Science and International Affairs, October 2018, http://belfercenter.org/publication/reflections -american-grand-strategy-asia; Douglas Feith and Gary Roughead, "China's Maritime Strategic Challenge," *National Review*, October 18, 2019, http://nationalreview.com /2019/10/china-maritime-threat-us-allies-must-work-together-to-meet-challenge; Andrew A. Michta, "As China Surges, Europe Is on the Menu," *American Interest*, September 11, 2019, http://the-american-interest.com/2019/09/11/as-china-surges -europe-is-on-the-menu; and Josh Rogin, "Trump and Europe Must Make Up and Work Together to Confront China," *Washington Post*, August 25, 2019, http:// washingtonpost.com/opinions/2019/08/25/trump-europe-must-make-up-work -together-confront-china.

113. Hyung-Jin Kim, "S. Korea Cancels Japan Intelligence Deal Amid Trade Dispute," Associated Press, August 22, 2019, http://apnews.com /b6f4856f55294c68a4f8228a45ddf362; Su-Hyun Lee and Ben Dooley, "Japan and South Korea Feud, but Breaking Up Is Hard," *New York Times*, August 28, 2019, http:// nytimes.com/2019/08/28/business/japan-south-korea-trade.html; and Motoko Rich, Edward Wong, and Choe Sang-Hun, "As Japan and South Korea Feud Intensifies, U.S. Seems Unwilling, or Unable, to Help," *New York Times*, August 4, 2019, http:// nytimes.com/2019/08/04/world/asia/japan-south-korea-feud.html.

114. Nevertheless, even without allies China receives periodic support in international organizations and multilateral forums from nations in Africa, the Middle East, and Southeast Asia.

115. Kissinger, *Years of Upheaval*, 853.

116. This recommendation draws heavily on Blackwill and Campbell, *Xi Jinping on the Global Stage*, and Blackwill and Tellis, *Revising U.S. Grand Strategy Toward China*. See Salvatore Babones, "America Must Pivot Toward China and Away From the Middle East," *National Interest*, May 1, 2019, http://nationalinterest.org/feature/america -must-pivot-toward-china-and-away-middle-east-55302; Michael Beckley, "The Emerging Military Balance in East Asia: How China's Neighbors Can Check Chinese Naval Expansion," *International Security* 52, no. 2 (2017): 78–119, http:// mitpressjournals.org/doi/pdfplus/10.1162/ISEC_a_00294; Hal Brands, "New U.S. Indo-Pacific Strategy Isn't Going to Scare China," Bloomberg, June 18, 2019, http:// bloomberg.com/opinion/articles/2019-06-18/u-s-indo-pacific-strategy-isn-t-going -to-scare-china; Brad Lendon, "China Could Overwhelm US Military in Asia in Hours, Australian Report Says," CNN, August 20, 2019, http://cnn.com/2019/08/20 /asia/australia-china-us-military-report-intl-hnk/index.html; Robert W. Merry, "The Great Power Game Is On and China Is Winning," *American Conservative*, May 22,

2019, http://theamericanconservative.com/articles/the-great-power-game-is-on-and
-china-is-winning; Mark Montgomery and Eric Sayers, "Addressing America's
Operational Shortfall in the Pacific," *War on the Rocks,* June 18, 2019, http://
warontherocks.com/2019/06/addressing-americas-operational-shortfall-in-the
-pacific; Missy Ryan and Dan Lamothe, "Defense Secretary Wants to Deliver on the
Goal of Outpacing China. Can He Do It?," *Washington Post,* August 6, 2019, http://
washingtonpost.com/world/national-security/defense-secretary-mark-esper-wants
-to-be-the-leader-who-finally-delivers-on-the-pentagons-goal-of-outpacing-china-can
-he-do-it/2019/08/06/671cacca-b86b-11e9-aeb2-a101a1fb27a7_story.html; and
Will Saetren and Hunter Marston, "Washington Must Own Up to Superpower
Competition With China," *Diplomat,* March 8, 2018, http://thediplomat.com/2018/03
/washington-must-own-up-to-superpower-competition-with-china.

117.   I am especially indebted to Admiral Gary Roughead for his many contributions to
       this section.

118.   For a visionary treatment of the U.S.-Japan alliance, see Richard L. Armitage and
       Joseph S. Nye, *The U.S.-Japan Alliance: Anchoring Stability in Asia* (Washington, DC:
       Center for Strategic and International Studies, 2012), 17, http://csis-prod.s3.amazonaws
       .com/s3fs-public/legacy_files/files/publication/120810_Armitage_USJapanAlliance
       _Web.pdf. Also see Michael J. Green and Nicholas Szechenyi, eds., *Pivot 2.0* (Washington,
       DC: Center for Strategic and International Studies, 2012), http://csis-prod.s3.amazonaws
       .com/s3fs-public/legacy_files/files/publication/141223_Green_Pivot_Web.pdf; Sheila
       Smith, "A Strategy for the U.S.-Japan Alliance," Council on Foreign Relations, April
       25, 2012, http://cfr.org/report/strategy-us-japan-alliance; and Sheila Smith, "Feeling
       the Heat: Asia's Shifting Geopolitics and the U.S.-Japan Alliance," *World Politics Review,*
       July 9, 2013, http://worldpoliticsreview.com/articles/13078/feeling-the-heat-asias
       -shifting-geopolitics-and-the-u-s-japan-alliance.

119.   International Monetary Fund, "GDP, Current Prices," IMF DataMapper, http://imf.org
       /external/datamapper/NGDPD@WEO/OEMDC/ADVEC/WEOWORLD/JPN;
       Tim Kelly, "Japan's Military Seek Eighth Straight Annual Hike in Defense Spending,"
       Reuters, August 30, 2019, http://reuters.com/article/us-japan-defence-budget/japans
       -military-seek-eighth-straight-annual-hike-in-defense-spending-idUSKCN1VK0D2;
       and U.S. Forces, Japan, "About USFJ," http://www.usfj.mil/About-USFJ.

120.   Australia, Canada, New Zealand, the United Kingdom, and the United States make up
       the Five Eyes. These countries cooperate in signals, military, and human intelligence.

121.   See Ellen Swicord, "The United States Needs Japan and South Korea to Make Up,"
       Diplomat, October 24, 2019, http://thediplomat.com/2019/10/the-united-states-needs
       -japan-and-south-korea-to-make-up.

122.   This is hardly the pattern of the Trump administration.

123.   See Swicord, "The United States Needs Japan and South Korea to Make Up."

124.   See Blackwill and Tellis, "The India Dividend," for an argument that the United States
       should treat India with "strategic altruism." See also Stratfor, "Wary of China, Modi
       Courts India's Neighbors," September 4, 2019, http://worldview.stratfor.com/article
       /wary-china-modi-courts-indias-neighbors-bri-china-infrastructure-belt-road.

125.   Murray Hiebert, Ted Osius, and Gregory B. Poling, *A U.S.-Indonesia Partnership for 2020:
       Recommendations for Forging a 21st Century Relationship* (Washington, DC: Center for

Strategic and International Studies, 2013), http://csis-prod.s3.amazonaws.com/s3fs
-public/legacy_files/files/publication/130917_Hiebert_USIndonesiaPartnership
_WEB.pdf.

126. Murray Hiebert, Phuong Nguyen, and Gregory B. Poling, "A New Era in U.S.-Vietnam
      Relations: Deepening Ties Two Decades After Normalization" (Washington, DC:
      Center for Strategic and International Studies, June 2014), http://csis-prod.s3.amazonaws
      .com/s3fs-public/legacy_files/files/publication/140609_Hiebert_USVietnamRelations
      _Web.pdf.

127. "U.S.-Burma Relations: Peace, Stability, and the Transition to Democracy," Policy
      Task Force, Henry M. Jackson School of International Studies, 2013, http://digital.lib
      .washington.edu/researchworks/bitstream/handle/1773/22745/TF%20D%202013
      .pdf?sequence=1&isAllowed=y.

128. Elizabeth Economy, *The Third Revolution: Xi Jinping and the New Chinese State* (New
      York: Oxford University Press, 2018), 247.

129. See Josh Rogin, "National Security Isn't a Bargaining Chip With China," *Washington
      Post*, July 26, 2019, http://washingtonpost.com/opinions/global-opinions/national
      -security-isnt-a-bargaining-chip-with-china/2019/07/25/ae609934-af1f-11e9-a0c9
      -6d2d7818f3da_story.html. For a summary of arguments for and against accelerating
      various aspects of the U.S. trade conflict with China, see Ishaan Tharoor, "Trump and Xi
      Lock Horns—and Drag the World With Them," *Washington Post*, August 7, 2019, http://
      washingtonpost.com/world/2019/08/07/trump-xi-lock-horns-drag-world-with-them.

130. Jim Zarroli, "China Churns Out Half the World's Steel, and Other Steelmakers Feel
      Pinched," NPR, March 8, 2018, http://npr.org/2018/03/08/591637097/china-churns
      -out-half-the-worlds-steel-and-other-steelmakers-feel-pinched.

131. Reuters, "Factbox—Barrier to Entry: China's Restrictions on U.S. Imports," March
      14, 2018, http://reuters.com/article/us-usa-trump-china-factbox/factbox-barrier-to
      -entry-chinas-restrictions-on-u-s-imports-idUSKCN1GQ0PQ.

132. Elizabeth Redden, "Stealing Innovation," *Inside Higher Ed*, April 29, 2019, http://
      insidehighered.com/news/2019/04/29/fbi-director-discusses-chinese-espionage
      -threat-us-academic-research.

133. Branstetter, "China's Forced Technology Transfer Problem—and What to Do About It."

134. "CrowdStrike Report Reveals Cyber Intrusion Trends From Elite Team of Threat
      Hunters," 2018, http://crowdstrike.com/resources/news/crowdstrike-report-reveals
      -cyber-intrusion-trends-from-elite-team-of-threat-hunters.

135. Nicole Perlroth, "Chinese and Iranian Hackers Renew Their Attacks on U.S.
      Companies," *New York Times*, February 18, 2019, http://nytimes.com/2019/02/18
      /technology/hackers-chinese-iran-usa.html.

136. See George Friedman, "The Geopolitical Logic of the US-China Trade War,"
      Geopolitical Futures, August 26, 2019, http://geopoliticalfutures.com/the-geopolitical
      -logic-of-the-us-china-trade-war.

137. David Brown, "The US and China Must End Their Trade War So the World Can Work
      Together to Restore Economic Order," *South China Morning Post*, March 18, 2019,
      http://scmp.com/comment/insight-opinion/united-states/article/3002122/us-and-china

-must-end-their-trade-war-so; John Dale Grover, "Stop the Trade War in the Name of Prosperity," *American Conservative*, September 16, 2019, http://theamericanconservative .com/articles/stop-the-trade-war-in-the-name-of-prosperity; and Gary Wolfram, "Time to End the Trade War," *Detroit News*, July 26, 2018, http://detroitnews.com/story /opinion/2018/07/27/time-end-trade-war/837112002.

138. Henry Kissinger, *Diplomacy* (New York: Simon & Schuster, 1994), 22–23.

139. There is, predictably and properly, a vigorous debate regarding how the United States should respond to the Hong Kong crisis. See Michael Crowley and Edward Wong, "Trump's Hong Kong Caution Isolates Him From Congress, Allies and Advisers," *New York Times*, August 15, 2019, http://nytimes.com/2019/08/15/us/politics/trump-hong -kong.html; David Ignatius, "The U.S. Has to Tread in the Middle When Handling the Hong Kong Protests," *Washington Post*, August 15, 2019, http://washingtonpost.com /opinions/global-opinions/the-us-has-to-tread-in-the-middle-when-handling-the-hong -kong-protests/2019/08/15/ee89b7b0-bf88-11e9-a5c6-1e74f7ec4a93_story.html; Eliana Johnson, Nahal Toosi, and Ben White, "Trump Resists Aides' Pressure to Back Hong Kong Protesters," *Politico*, August 14, 2019, http://politico.com/story/2019/08 /14/trump-hong-kong-protesters-1463605; and Ishaan Tharoor, "U.S. Politicians Embrace Hong Kong's Struggle, Raising the Stakes for China," *Washington Post*, September 18, 2019, http://washingtonpost.com/world/2019/09/18/us-politicians -embrace-hong-kongs-struggle-raising-stakes-china. For proponents of increased pressure in response to China's human rights abuses, see Editorial Board, "Why Redefine U.S. Policy on Human Rights?," *Washington Post*, August 23, 2019, http:// washingtonpost.com/opinions/global-opinions/why-redefine-us-policy-on-human -rights/2019/08/23/d570aadc-a33f-11e9-b732-41a79c2551bf_story.html; Michael Mazza, "US-China Great Power Competition: The Role of Values, Hong Kong, and Taiwan," *Global Taiwan Brief* (blog), August 14, 2019, http://globaltaiwan.org/2019 /08/vol-4-issue-16/#MichaelMazza08142019; Shane McCrum and Olivia Enos, "China's Worsening Human Rights Abuses Mimic Mao," *Daily Signal*, May 13, 2019, http://dailysignal.com/2019/05/13/chinas-worsening-human-rights-abuses-evoke -memories-of-mao; Ishaan Tharoor, "Hong Kong's Protests Flare in the Shadow of the U.S.-China Rivalry," *Washington Post*, July 29, 2019, http://washingtonpost.com /world/2019/07/29/hong-kongs-protests-flare-shadow-us-china-rivalry; Marc A. Thiessen, "China Does Not Have the Upper Hand in Hong Kong. Trump Does," *Washington Post*, August 15, 2019, http://washingtonpost.com/opinions/2019/08/15 /china-does-not-have-upper-hand-hong-kong-trump-does; Marco Rubio, "Marco Rubio: China Is Showing Its True Nature in Hong Kong. The U.S. Must Not Watch From the Sidelines," *Washington Post*, September 3, 2019, http://washingtonpost.com /opinions/global-opinions/marco-rubio-china-must-respect-hong-kongs-autonomy--or -face-the-consequences/2019/09/03/7399e69a-ce80-11e9-b29b-a528dc82154a _story.html; and Elizabeth Warren, "It Is Time for the United States to Stand Up to China in Hong Kong," *Foreign Policy*, October 3, 2019, http://foreignpolicy.com/2019 /10/03/it-is-time-for-the-united-states-to-stand-up-to-china-in-hong-kong. See also Keith Bradsher, "Why the Protests in Hong Kong May Have No End in Sight," *New York Times*, October 17, 2019, http://nytimes.com/2019/10/17/world/asia/hong -kong-protests.html; Anna Fifield, "China's Ominous Warning to Hong Kong: Less Tolerance, More Patriotic Education," *Washington Post*, November 1, 2019, http://washingtonpost.com/world/asia_pacific/chinas-ominous-warning-to-hong

-kong-less-tolerance-more-patriotic-education/2019/11/01/bbdc4edc-fc72-11e9
-9e02-1d45cb3dfa8f_story.html; Thomas L. Friedman, "Hong Kong's Protests
Could Be Another Social Media Revolution That Ends in Failure," *New York Times*,
September 17, 2019, http://nytimes.com/2019/09/17/opinion/hong-kong-protest
.html; David Ignatius, "Are Hong Kong's Protesters Headed Toward an Arab Spring
Ending?," *Washington Post*, September 17, 2019, http://washingtonpost.com/opinions
/global-opinions/are-hong-kongs-protesters-headed-toward-an-arab-spring-ending
/2019/09/17/2d20d9be-d96e-11e9-a688-303693fb4b0b_story.html; Shibani
Mahtani, "Hong Kong Activists Press U.S. to Counter China's Erosion of City's
Freedoms," *Washington Post*, September 17, 2019, http://washingtonpost.com/world
/asia_pacific/hong-kong-activists-press-us-to-counter-chinas-erosion-of-citys-freedoms
/2019/09/17/99a7d542-d8fb-11e9-a1a5-162b8a9c9ca2_story.html; Steven Lee
Myers, "China Hints Its Troops Could Be Used to Quell Hong Kong Protests," *New
York Times*, July 24, 2019, http://nytimes.com/2019/07/24/world/asia/china-military-
hong-kong-taiwan-protests.html; Evan Osnos, "China's Hong Kong Dilemma," *New
Yorker*, August 25, 2019, http://newyorker.com/magazine/2019/09/02/chinas-hong
-kong-dilemma; Tao Peng, "Beijing's Strategic Anxiety and Growing Tactical Offensive
Under the Ultimate Pressure of the U.S.," *RealClearDefense*, August 2, 2019, http://
realcleardefense.com/articles/2019/08/02/beijings_strategic_anxiety_and_growing
_tactical_offensive_under_the_ultimate_pressure_of_the_us_114633.html; Jane
Perlez, "China Reacts to Trade Tariffs and Hong Kong Protests by Blaming U.S.," *New
York Times*, August 2, 2019, http://nytimes.com/2019/08/02/world/asia/china-trump
.html; Stratfor, "Hong Kong, U.S.: Committee Approves Democracy Bill, Angering
China," September 26, 2019, http://worldview.stratfor.com/situation-report/hong
-kong-us-committee-approves-democracy-bill-angering-china; Lewis Lau Yiu-man,
"Hong Kong and the Independence Movement That Doesn't Know Itself," *New York
Times*, September 27, 2019, http://nytimes.com/2019/09/27/opinion/hong-kong
-umbrella.html; and George F. Will, "Hong Kong Is a 'Hair's Breadth From Destruction,'" *Washington Post*, September 13, 2019, http://washingtonpost.com/opinions
/global-opinions/hong-kong-is-a-hairs-breadth-from-destruction/2019/09/13
/fa96121c-d57a-11e9-9343-40db57cf6abd_story.html.

140. Timothy McLaughlin and Casey Quackenbush, "Hong Kong Protesters Sing 'Star-
Spangled Banner,' Call on Trump to 'Liberate' the City," *Washington Post*, September
8, 2019, http://washingtonpost.com/world/hong-kong-protesters-call-on-trump-to
-liberate-hong-kong/2019/09/08/4123008c-d215-11e9-9610-fb56c5522e1c_story
.html. See also Edward Wong, "Hong Kong Protesters Call for U.S. Help. China Sees a
Conspiracy.," *New York Times*, November 3, 2019, http://nytimes.com/2019/11/03
/world/asia/hong-kong-protesters-call-for-us-help-china-sees-a-conspiracy.html.

141. See Gary Schmitt, "China Is Quietly Winning the Diplomatic War With Taiwan," *Hill*,
September 26, 2019, http://thehill.com/opinion/international/463290-china-is
-quietly-winning-the-diplomatic-war-with-taiwan; and George F. Will, "What Hong
Kong's Resistance Means for Taiwan," *Washington Post*, September 20, 2019, http://
washingtonpost.com/opinions/global-opinions/what-hong-kongs-resistance-means
-for-taiwan/2019/09/20/c0f3a3cc-db0f-11e9-ac63-3016711543fe_story.html.

142. See Allison, *Destined for War*; Chris Buckley and Chris Horton, "Xi Jinping Warns
Taiwan That Unification Is the Goal and Force Is an Option," *New York Times*, January
1, 2019, http://nytimes.com/2019/01/01/world/asia/xi-jinping-taiwan-china.html;

Derek Grossman, "No Smiles Across the Taiwan Strait," *Foreign Policy*, January 9, 2019, http://foreignpolicy.com/2019/01/07/no-smiles-across-the-taiwan-strait; Nicholas Kristof, "This Is How a War With China Could Begin," *New York Times*, September 4, 2019, http://nytimes.com/2019/09/04/opinion/china-taiwan-war.html; Michael Mazza, "Is a Storm Brewing in the Taiwan Strait?," *Foreign Affairs*, July 27, 2018, http://foreignaffairs.com/articles/asia/2018-07-27/storm-brewing-taiwan-strait; Peng, "Beijing's Strategic Anxiety and Growing Tactical Offensive Under the Ultimate Pressure of the U.S."; John Pomfret, "China's Xi Jinping Is Growing Impatient With Taiwan, Adding to Tensions With U.S.," *Washington Post*, February 18, 2019, http://washingtonpost.com/opinions/2019/02/18/chinas-xi-jinping-is-growing-impatient-with-taiwan-adding-tensions-with-united-states; and Gerry Shih, "China Takes Aim at U.S. and Taiwan in New Military Blueprint," *Washington Post*, July 24, 2019, http://washingtonpost.com/world/china-takes-aim-at-us-taiwan-in-new-military-blueprint/2019/07/24/38168b14-adbf-11e9-9411-a608f9d0c2d3_story.html. See also Eric Heginbotham and Rajan Menon, "Taiwan's Balancing Act," *National Interest*, February 11, 2019, http://nationalinterest.org/feature/taiwans-balancing-act-44247.

143. Edward Wong, "Trump Administration Approves F-16 Fighter Jet Sales to Taiwan," *New York Times*, August 16, 2019, http://nytimes.com/2019/08/16/world/asia/taiwan-f16.html. See Ralph Jennings, "Trump plans to ship a fleet of F-16s to Taiwan. China isn't happy about it," *Los Angeles Times*, August 19, 2019, http://latimes.com/world-nation/story/2019-08-19/trump-plans-to-ship-a-fleet-off-16s-to-taiwan-and-china-isnt-happy-about-it; and Sean Lin, "Ma Bashes Tsai for US Foreign Policy," *Taipei Times*, October 6, 2019, http://taipeitimes.com/News/taiwan/archives/2019/10/06/2003723475.

144. Kristof, "This Is How a War With China Could Begin."

145. There is no better public source on cyber issues than David Sanger's frequent revelations on the front page of the *New York Times*.

146. Jonathan Masters, "Confronting the Cyber Threat," Council on Foreign Relations, May 23, 2011, http://cfr.org/backgrounder/confronting-cyber-threat. For compelling conceptual examinations of cyber issues, see Joseph S. Nye Jr., "Cyberspace Wars," *New York Times*, February 27, 2011, http://nytimes.com/2011/02/28/opinion/28iht-ednye28.html; Joseph S. Nye Jr., "Deterrence and Dissuasion in Cyberspace," *International Security* 41, no. 3 (Winter 2016/2017): 44–71; and Joseph S. Nye Jr., "The World Needs New Norms on Cyberwarfare," *Washington Post*, October 1, 2015, http://washingtonpost.com/opinions/the-world-needs-an-arms-control-treaty-for-cybersecurity/2015/10/01/20c3e970-66dd-11e5-9223-70cb36460919_story.html.

147. See Lorand Laskai and Adam Segal, "A New Old Threat: Countering the Return of Chinese Industrial Cyber Espionage," Council on Foreign Relations, December 6, 2018, http://cfr.org/report/threat-chinese-espionage; and Zack Cooper and Eric B. Lorber, "The Right Way to Sanction China," *National Interest*, February 23, 2016, http://nationalinterest.org/feature/the-right-way-sanction-china-15285. For an examination of the perils of sanctions combined with poor attribution strategies, see Sandeep Baliga, Ethan Bueno de Mesquita, and Alexander Wolitzky, "The Case for a Cyber Deterrence Plan That Works," *National Interest*, March 5, 2019, http://nationalinterest.org/feature/case-cyber-deterrence-plan-works-46207.

148. Del Quentin Wilber, "China 'Has Taken the Gloves Off' in Its Thefts of U.S. Technology Secrets," *Los Angeles Times,* November 16, 2018, http://latimes.com /politics/la-na-pol-china-economic-espionage-20181116-story.html; Jeff Daniels, "Chinese Theft of Sensitive US Military Technology Is Still a 'Huge Problem,' Says Defense Analyst," CNBC, November 9, 2017, http://cnbc.com/2017/11/08 /chinese-theft-of-sensitive-us-military-technology-still-huge-problem.html; and Ellen Nakashima, "Chinese Breach Data of 4 Million Federal Workers," *Washington Post,* June 4, 2015, http://washingtonpost.com/world/national-security/chinese-hackers -breach-federal-governments-personnel-office/2015/06/04/889c0e52-0af7-11e5 -95fd-d580f1c5d44e_story.html.

149. Laskai and Segal, "A New Old Threat."

150. Jack Goldsmith and Robert D. Williams, "The Failure of the United States' Chinese-Hacking Indictment Strategy," *Lawfare* (blog), December 28, 2018, http://lawfareblog .com/failure-united-states-chinese-hacking-indictment-strategy.

151. See Laskai and Segal, "A New Old Threat"; and Goldsmith and Williams, "The Failure of the United States' Chinese-Hacking Indictment Strategy."

152. See Michele Flournoy and Michael Sulmeyer, "Battlefield Internet," *Foreign Affairs,* September/October 2019, http://foreignaffairs.com/articles/world/2018-08-14 /battlefield-internet; and Nina Kollars and Jacquelyn Schneider, "Defending Forward: The 2018 Cyber Strategy Is Here," *War on the Rocks,* September 20, 2018, http:// warontherocks.com/2018/09/defending-forward-the-2018-cyber-strategy-is-here.

153. See Erica D. Borghard and Shawn W. Lonergan, "Chinese Hackers Are Stealing U.S. Defense Secrets: Here Is How to Stop Them," Council on Foreign Relations, March 11, 2019, http://cfr.org/blog/chinese-hackers-are-stealing-us-defense-secrets-here -how-stop-them. In this regard, former National Security Advisor John Bolton is right that the purpose of a more robust offensive strategy is to tell other nations carrying out cyber operations against the United States that Washington will "impose costs on you until you get the point that it's not worth your while to use cyber against us." See John Bolton, "*Wall Street Journal* CFO Conference," interview by John Bussey, CSPAN, http://c-span.org/video/?461598-2/john-bolton-speaks-wall-street-journal -cfo-conference.

154. Ariel Levite and Lyu Jinghua, "Chinese-American Relations in Cyberspace: Toward Collaboration or Confrontation?," Carnegie Endowment for International Peace, January 24, 2019, http://carnegieendowment.org/2019/01/24/chinese-american -relations-in-cyberspace-toward-collaboration-or-confrontation-pub-78213.

155. See Scott W. Harold, Martin C. Libicki, and Astrid Stuth Cevallos, *Getting to Yes With China in Cyberspace* (Santa Monica, CA: RAND Corporation, 2016), 70–75, http:// rand.org/pubs/research_reports/RR1335.html.

156. See Sarah Cook and Annie Boyajian, "How the US Government Can Counter China's Growing Media Influence," *Hill,* June 6, 2019, http://thehill.com/opinion/civil-rights /446998-how-the-us-government-can-counter-chinas-growing-media-influence; Larry Diamond and Orville Schell, *Chinese Influence and American Interests: Promoting Constructive Vigilance* (Stanford, CA: Hoover Institution Press, 2018), http://hoover.org /sites/default/files/research/docs/chineseinfluence_americaninterests_fullreport _web.pdf; and Tanner Greer, "Can American Values Survive in a Chinese World?,"

Foreign Policy, October 12, 2019, http://foreignpolicy.com/2019/10/12/american-values-survive-chinese-world-xi-jinping. For further insight into Beijing's influence campaigns in the United States and abroad, see Michael Birnbaum, "China Is Investing in Europe—but There Are Strings Attached," *Washington Post*, August 19, 2019, http://washingtonpost.com/world/europe/china-is-investing-in-europe--but-there-are-strings-attached/2019/08/18/35407f32-b2d1-11e9-acc8-1d847bacca73_story.html; Editorial Board, "There's Another Expert Player Warming Up to Online Election Interference. We Should Worry," *Washington Post*, September 22, 2019, http://washingtonpost.com/opinions/global-opinions/theres-another-expert-player-warming-up-to-online-election-interference-we-should-worry/2019/09/22/76c8c870-d990-11e9-bfb1-849887369476_story.html; Louisa Lim, "The Battle for Hong Kong Is Being Fought in Sydney and Vancouver," *New York Times,* August 13, 2019, http://nytimes.com/2019/08/13/opinion/hong-kong-protests.html; Donie O'Sullivan, "How a Hacked American Nightclub Twitter Account Was Implicated in China's Information War," CNN, August 21, 2019, http://cnn.com/2019/08/20/tech/twitter-china-us/index.html; Josh Rogin, "China's Efforts to Undermine Democracy Are Expanding Worldwide," *Washington Post,* June 27, 2019, http://washingtonpost.com/opinions/2019/06/27/chinas-efforts-undermine-democracy-are-expanding-worldwide; and Vuk Vuksanovic, "Light Touch, Tight Grip: China's Influence and the Corrosion of Serbian Democracy," *War on the Rocks*, September 24, 2019, http://warontherocks.com/2019/09/light-touch-tight-grip-chinas-influence-and-the-corrosion-of-serbian-democracy. For further suggestions on how to counter foreign influence campaigns in the United States, see David L. Sloss, "Corporate Defenses Against Information Warfare," Just Security, August 20, 2019, http://justsecurity.org/65826/corporate-defenses-against-information-warfare.

157. Sui-Lee Wee, "Giving In to China, U.S. Airlines Drop Taiwan (in Name at Least)," *New York Times*, July 25, 2019, http://nytimes.com/2018/07/25/business/taiwan-american-airlines-china.html; O'Sullivan, "How a Hacked American Nightclub Twitter Account Was Implicated in China's Information War"; and Diamond and Schell, *Chinese Influence and American Interests: Promoting Constructive Vigilance.* See also Edward Wong, "Pence Says U.S. Companies Leave 'Conscience at the Door' Over China," *New York Times*, October 24, 2019, http://nytimes.com/2019/10/24/us/politics/pence-china-hong-kong-nba.html.

158. I am indebted to Research Associate Daniel Clay for his encyclopedic command of this issue. Riley Griffin and Eben Novy-Williams, "NBA's Adam Silver Says Crisis in China Triggered 'Substantial' Losses," Bloomberg, October 17, 2019, http://bloomberg.com/news/articles/2019-10-17/nba-s-silver-says-crisis-in-china-triggered-substantial-losses; Sopan Deb, "Chinese State Television Vows 'Retribution' Against N.B.A.'s Adam Silver," *New York Times*, October 19, 2019, http://nytimes.com/2019/10/19/sports/basketball/nba-china-adam-silver-retribution.html; and Ryan Woo and David Stanway, "Houston Rockets Nike Merchandise Disappears From China Stores," Reuters, October 10, 2019, http://reuters.com/article/us-china-basketball-nba-nike-idUSKBN1WP109.

159. John Gonzalez, "Daryl Morey's Hong Kong Tweet Has Put His Relationship With the Rockets in Limbo," Ringer, October 6, 2019, http://theringer.com/nba/2019/10/6/20901828/daryl-morey-hong-kong-china-houston-rockets-tweet-controversy. For further commentary on the aftermath of Morey's tweet, see BBC News, "Mike Pence

Criticises NBA as 'Wholly-Owned Subsidiary' of China," October 25, 2019, http://
bbc.com/news/world-us-canada-50171698; Editorial Board, "The Chinese Threat to
American Free Speech," *New York Times*, October 19, 2019, http://nytimes.com/2019
/10/19/opinion/sunday/china-nba.html; Ben Sasse, "China Is Waging War With
U.S. Businesses. And It's Winning," *Washington Post*, October 13, 2019, http://
washingtonpost.com/opinions/global-opinions/china-is-waging-war-with-us
-businesses-and-its-winning/2019/10/13/fe676c8e-ed02-11e9-85c0-85a098e47b37
_story.html; and Mimi Lee, "How NBA Fans Can Respond to the League's Dismissal
of Hong Kong," *Washington Post*, October 21, 2019, http://washingtonpost.com
/opinions/global-opinions/why-ill-be-handing-out-shirts-in-support-of-hong-kong
-before-the-start-of-the-nba-season/2019/10/21/b3180302-f422-11e9-8cf0
-4cc99f74d127_story.html.

160. See Larry Diamond and Orville Schell's convincing book *Chinese Influence and
American Interests*; and Peter Mattis and Alex Joske, "The Third Magic Weapon:
Reforming China's United Front," *War on the Rocks*, June 24, 2019, http://
warontherocks.com/2019/06/the-third-magic-weapon-reforming-chinas-united-front.

161. Gerry Shih, "Ambassador, Defending New Rules, Says China Has Obstructed
U.S. Diplomats' Work for Decades," *Washington Post*, October 21, 2019, http://
washingtonpost.com/world/asia_pacific/ambassador-defending-new-rules-says-china
-has-obstructed-us-diplomats-work-for-decades/2019/10/21/9ae51e96-f3b9-11e9
-b2d2-1f37c9d82dbb_story.html.

162. For views here, see Diamond and Schell, *Chinese Influence and American Interests*, 36.

163. See Diamond and Schell, *Chinese Influence and American Interests*, 50, 77.

164. See Diamond and Schell, *Chinese Influence and American Interests*, XX, 77.

165. See Diamond and Schell, *Chinese Influence and American Interests*, 25–26.

166. See Paul Mozur, "Live From America's Capital, a TV Station Run by China's
Communist Party," *New York Times*, February 28, 2019, http://nytimes.com/2019/02/28
/business/cctv-china-usa-propaganda.html; and Daniel Wagner, "China Is Waging a
Silent Media War for Global Influence," *National Interest*, September 19, 2019, http://
nationalinterest.org/feature/china-waging-silent-media-war-global-influence-81906.

167. For concurring views, see Cook and Boyajian, "How the US Government Can
Counter China's Growing Media Influence."

168. In our book *War by Other Means*, Jennifer Harris and I define geoeconomics as "the
use of economic instruments to promote and defend national interests and to produce
beneficial geopolitical results, and the effects of other nations' economic actions on
a country's geopolitical goals" (9). Much of this recommendation first appeared in
Robert D. Blackwill, "Indo-Pacific Strategy in an Era of Geoeconomics" (keynote
speech, conference sponsored by the Japan Forum on International Relations, Tokyo,
Japan, July 31, 2018), http://cdn.cfr.org/sites/default/files/pdf/8-20%20Tokyo%20
Presentation.pdf.

169. See Blackwill and Harris, *War by Other Means*; Peter Harrell, Elizabeth Rosenberg, and
Edoardo Saravalle, "China's Use of Coercive Economic Measures," Center for a New
American Security, June 2018, http://s3.amazonaws.com/files.cnas.org/documents
/China_Use_FINAL-1.pdf?mtime=20180604161240; Evan Karlik, "China Will Use

Economic Pain to Hinder US's Pacific Missile Deployment," *Nikkei Asian Review*, October 4, 2019, http://asia.nikkei.com/Opinion/China-will-use-economic-pain-to -hinder-US-s-Pacific-missile-deployment; Catherine Wong, "'Don't Ignore China's Economic Coercion': Former Clinton Aide's Advice to Next US President," *South China Morning Post*, September 29, 2016, http://scmp.com/news/china/diplomacy -defence/article/2023342/dont-ignore-beijings-economic-coercion-advice-next-us; and Ketian Vivian Zhang, "Chinese Non-military Coercion—Tactics and Rationale," Brookings Institution, January 22, 2019, http://brookings.edu/articles/chinese-non -military-coercion-tactics-and-rationale.

170. See Blackwill and Harris, "Geoeconomics in Chinese Foreign Policy," chapter 4 in *War by Other Means*. For statistics on U.S. allies' trading partners, see World Integrated Trade Solution, "Australia Trade Summary," accessed September 11, 2019, http:// wits.worldbank.org/CountryProfile/en/Country/AUS/Year/2017/Summary; World Integrated Trade Solution, "Japan Trade Summary," accessed September 11, 2019, http://wits.worldbank.org/CountryProfile/en/Country/JPN/Year/2017/Summary; and World Integrated Trade Solution, "Korea, Rep. Trade Summary," accessed September 11, 2019, http://wits.worldbank.org/CountryProfile/en/Country/KOR /Year/LTST/Summary.

171. See Niruban Balachandran, "The United States Should Join the Asian Infrastructure Investment Bank," *Asia Pacific Bulletin* no. 397, East-West Center, September 20, 2017, http://eastwestcenter.org/system/tdf/private/apb397.pdf?file=1&type=node&id =36284; and Leland Lazarus, "Why the US Should Embrace the AIIB," *Diplomat*, March 2, 2016, http://thediplomat.com/2016/03/why-the-u-s-should-embrace-the-aiib.

172. Tamar Gutner, "AIIB: Is the Chinese-Led Development Bank a Role Model?," Council on Foreign Relations, June 25, 2018, http://cfr.org/blog/aiib-chinese-led-development -bank-role-model.

173. Asian Infrastructure Investment Bank, Articles of Agreement of the Asian Infrastructure Investment Bank, 2015, Article 31, http://aiib.org/en/about-aiib/basic-documents /_download/articles-of-agreement/basic_document_english-bank_articles_of _agreement.pdf.

174. See Blackwill and Harris, *War by Other Means*.

175. The Trump administration has taken the opposite approach and unwisely withdrew from the Paris climate agreement, the United Nations' cultural organization, and the UN Human Rights Council, and pulled funding from the UN Relief and Works Agency, which helps Palestinian refugees. Michael D. Shear, "Trump Will Withdraw U.S. From Paris Climate Agreement," *New York Times*, June 1, 2017, http://nytimes.com/2017/06 /01/climate/trump-paris-climate-agreement.html; Eli Rosenberg and Carol Morello, "U.S. Withdraws From UNESCO, the U.N.'s Cultural Organization, Citing Anti-Israel Bias," *Washington Post*, October 12, 2017, http://washingtonpost.com/news/post-nation /wp/2017/10/12/u-s-withdraws-from-unesco-the-u-n-s-cultural-organization-citing -anti-israel-bias; Carol Morello, "U.S. Withdraws From U.N. Human Rights Council Over Perceived Bias Against Israel," *Washington Post*, June 19, 2018, http:// washingtonpost.com/world/national-security/us-expected-to-back-away-from-un -human-rights-council/2018/06/19/a49c2d0c-733c-11e8-b4b7-308400242c2e_story .html; and Karen DeYoung, Ruth Eglash, and Hazem Balousha, "U.S. Ends Aid to United Nations Agency Supporting Palestinian Refugees," *Washington Post*, August 31,

2018, http://washingtonpost.com/world/middle_east/us-aid-cuts-wont-end-the-right
-of-return-palestinians-say/2018/08/31/8e3f25b4-ad0c-11e8-8a0c-70b618c98d3c
_story.html. See also Andrea Kendall-Taylor and Rachel Rizzo, "The U.S. or China?
Europe Needs to Pick a Side," *Politico*, August 12, 2019, http://politico.com/magazine
/story/2019/08/12/us-china-europe-relations-227614; Colum Lynch and Robbie
Gramer, "Outfoxed and Outgunned: How China Routed the U.S. in a U.N. Agency,"
Foreign Policy, October 23, 2019, http://foreignpolicy.com/2019/10/23/china-united
-states-fao-kevin-moley; and Stephen M. Walt, "Yesterday's Cold War Shows How to
Beat China Today," *Foreign Policy*, July 29, 2019, http://foreignpolicy.com/2019/07/29
/yesterdays-cold-war-shows-how-to-beat-china-today.

176.   See Philip Zelikow and Condoleezza Rice, *To Build a Better World: Choices to End
the Cold War and Create a Global Commonwealth* (New York: Grand Central
Publishing, 2019).

177.   For an analysis of Putin's Russia, see Susan B. Glasser, "Putin the Great," *Foreign
Affairs*, September/October 2019, http://foreignaffairs.com/articles/russian-federation
/2019-08-12/putin-great.

178.   See Graham Allison, "China and Russia: A Strategic Alliance in the Making," *National
Interest*, December 14, 2018, http://nationalinterest.org/feature/china-and-russia
-strategic-alliance-making-38727; and George S. Beebe, *The Russia Trap: How Our
Shadow War With Russia Could Spiral Into Nuclear Catastrophe* (New York: Thomas
Dunne Books, St. Martin's Press, 2019). Not everyone agrees with Allison. See Nyshka
Chandran, "'Serious' Rivalry Still Drives China-Russia Relations Despite Improving
Ties," CNBC, September 14, 2018, http://cnbc.com/2018/09/14/china-russia-ties
--more-rivalry-than-allaince.html; and Yacqub Ismail, "The Limits of the Alliance
Between China and Russia," *National Interest*, July 10, 2019, http://nationalinterest.org
/feature/limits-alliance-between-china-and-russia-66406.

179.   For steps to this end, see Joshua A. Geltzer, "The 2 Steps to Fix Relations With Russia,"
Foreign Policy, July 29, 2019, http://foreignpolicy.com/2019/07/29/the-2-steps-to-fix
-relations-with-russia; and Dimitri K. Simes, "Delusions About Russia," *National
Interest*, August 8, 2019, http://nationalinterest.org/feature/delusions-about-russia
-72321. For a summary of the risks associated with deteriorating U.S.-Russia
relations, see Beebe, *The Russia Trap*.

180.   See Van Jackson, "Risk Realism: The Arms Control Endgame for North Korea Policy,"
Center for a New American Security, September 24, 2019, http://cnas.org
/publications/reports/risk-realism; and Caitlin Oprysko, "Bolton Undercuts Trump
and Says North Korea Has No Desire to Give Up Its Nukes," *Politico*, September 30,
2019, http://politico.com/news/2019/09/30/john-bolton-north-korea-nukes-011658.

181.   See Patrick Cronin, "Could North Korea Help Bring the United States and China
Closer Together?" *Foreign Policy*, May 4, 2018, http://foreignpolicy.com/2018/05/04
/could-north-korea-help-bring-the-united-states-and-china-closer-together; Wang
Junsheng, "US-China Cooperation Vital for the Success of Trump-Kim Summit,"
Atlantic Council, June 11, 2018, http://atlanticcouncil.org/blogs/new-atlanticist/us
-china-cooperation-vital-for-the-success-of-trump-kim-summit; and U.S. Institute of
Peace China-North Korea Senior Study Group, "China's Role in North Korea Nuclear
and Peace Negotiations" (Washington, DC: USIP, 2019), http://usip.org/publications
/2019/05/chinas-role-north-korea-nuclear-and-peace-negotiations.

182. See John Power and Catherine Wong, "Exclusive Details and Footage Emerge of Near Collision Between Warships in South China Sea," *South China Morning Post,* November 4, 2018, http://scmp.com/week-asia/geopolitics/article/2171596/exclusive -details-and-footage-emerge-near-collision-between.

183. Lyle J. Morris, "Time to Speak Up About the South China Sea," RAND Corporation, March 20, 2019, http://rand.org/blog/2019/03/time-to-speak-up-about-the-south -china-sea.html; Richard Heydarian, "How the Scarborough Shoal Came Back to Haunt China-Philippines Relations," *South China Morning Post,* July 23, 2018, http:// scmp.com/news/china/diplomacy-defence/article/2151923/how-scarborough-shoal -came-back-haunt-china-philippines; Gregory Poling and Bonnie S. Glaser, "How the U.S. Can Step Up in the South China Sea: The Right Way to Push Back Against Beijing," *Foreign Affairs,* January 16, 2019, http://foreignaffairs.com/articles/china /2019-01-16/how-us-can-step-south-china-sea; and "China Lands First Bomber On South China Sea Island," CSIS, May 18, 2018, http://amti.csis.org/china-lands-first -bomber-south-china-sea-island.

184. For concurring views, see Michael H. Fuchs, "Safe Harbor: How to End the South China Sea Crisis," *Foreign Affairs,* March 2, 2016, http://foreignaffairs.com/articles /china/2016-03-02/safe-harbor; and Ely Ratner, "Course Correction: How to Stop China's Maritime Advance," *Foreign Affairs,* July/August 2017, http://foreignaffairs .com/articles/2017-06-13/course-correction.

185. See Ratner, "Course Correction: How to Stop China's Maritime Advance."

186. See Poling and Glaser, "How the U.S. Can Step Up in the South China Sea."

187. See Ratner, "Course Correction: How to Stop China's Maritime Advance."

188. Special thanks to CFR colleague Amy Myers Jaffe for her comments and suggestions in this section.

189. Somini Sengupta, "U.S.-China Friction Threatens to Undercut the Fight Against Climate Change," *New York Times,* December 7, 2018, http://nytimes.com/2018/12 /07/climate/us-china-climate-change.html.

190. See Feng Hao, "Obama's Former Science Chief Looks to China for Climate Leadership," China Dialogue, September 20, 2019, http://chinadialogue.net/article /show/single/en/11526-John-Holdren-on-China-s-climate-leadership.

191. See Hart and Magsamen, "Limit, Leverage, and Compete," 25. For information on China's BRI activity, see Sagatom Saha, "China's Belt and Road Plan Is Destroying the World," *National Interest,* August 18, 2019, http://nationalinterest.org/feature/chinas -belt-and-road-plan-destroying-world-74166.

192. See Joseph Aldy et al., "Bilateral Cooperation Between China and the United States: Facilitating Progress on Climate-Change Policy," Belfer Center for Science and International Affairs, February 2016, 14–20, http://belfercenter.org/sites/default/files /files/publication/harvard-nscs-paper-final-160224.pdf.

193. See Joanna Lewis, "The U.S.-China Climate and Energy Relationship," *Parallel Perspectives on the Global Economic Order,* Center for Strategic and International Studies, September 2017, http://csis.org/us-china-climate-and-energy-relationship.

194. See Aldy et al., "Bilateral Cooperation Between China and the United States," 22. For information on climate capture technology, see John Schwartz, "Can Carbon Capture

Technology Prosper Under Trump?," *New York Times*, January 2, 2017, http://nytimes
.com/2017/01/02/science/donald-trump-carbon-capture-clean-coal.html.

195. Amy Myers Jaffe, "Green Giant: Renewable Energy and Chinese Power," *Foreign Affairs*,
      March/April 2018, http://foreignaffairs.com/articles/china/2018-02-13/green-giant.

196. Stephen Chen, "China Needs More Water. So It's Building a Rain-Making Network
      Three Times the Size of Spain," *South China Morning Post*, March 26, 2018, http://
      scmp.com/news/china/society/article/2138866/china-needs-more-water-so-its
      -building-rain-making-network-three.

197. Jaffe, "Green Giant."

198. For views similar to those expressed in this paragraph, see Jaffe, "Green Giant."

199. See Jaffe, "Green Giant."

200. Katrina Yu and Dan Sagalyn, "How China Is Driving the Future of Electric Cars,"
      PBS, October 2, 2019, http://pbs.org/newshour/show/how-china-is-driving-the-future
      -of-electric-cars; and Coral Davenport, "Automakers Plan for Their Worst Nightmare:
      Regulatory Chaos After Trump's Emissions Rollback," *New York Times*, April 10, 2019,
      http://nytimes.com/2019/04/10/climate/auto-emissions-cafe-rollback-trump.html.

201. Aldy et al., "Bilateral Cooperation Between China and the United States," 10–13; Kelley
      Hamrick, "California Moves With Chinese Provinces on Climate," *AnthropoZine*, http://
      anthropozine.com/uncategorized/california-moves-with-chinese-provinces-on
      -climate; and Valerie Volcovici, "California Ex-Governor Launches Climate Partnership
      With China," Reuters, September 23, 2019, http://reuters.com/article/us-climate
      -change-un-china/california-ex-governor-launches-climate-partnership-with-china
      -idUSKBN1W82A6.

202. The classic work on the characteristics of Chinese diplomacy is Henry Kissinger's
      On China (New York: Penguin, 2011). Kissinger makes a broader point in *Years of
      Upheaval* regarding diplomatic success, which should be applied to the U.S. approach
      to China: "From my study of history I was convinced that the period just after any
      diplomatic victory is frequently the most precarious. The victor is tempted to turn
      the screw one time too many; the loser, rubbed raw by the humiliation of his defeat,
      may be so eager to recoup that he suddenly abandons rational calculation." Kissinger,
      Years of Upheaval, 606. See also Kevin Rudd's thoughtful *U.S.-China 21: The Future of
      U.S.-China Relations Under Xi Jinping* (Cambridge, MA: Belfer Center for Science and
      International Affairs, 2015); "China's Political Economy Into 2020" (speech, London,
      July 11, 2019); his many other more recent publications on the subject; and Graham
      Allison, "Could the United States and China Be Rivalry Partners?" *National Interest*,
      July 7, 2019, http://nationalinterest.org/feature/could-united-states-and-china-be
      -rivalry-partners-65661. Portions of this recommendation first appeared in Blackwill,
      Trump's Foreign Policies Are Better Than They Seem and Blackwill, "Managing the U.S.-
      China Great Power Relationship."

203. See Richard McGregor, "Trump Wants China to Help Him Win. China Wants
      Nothing to Do With Him," *Washington Post*, October 11, 2019, http://washingtonpost
      .com/outlook/trump-wants-china-to-help-him-win-china-wants-nothing-to-do-with
      -him/2019/10/10/15fddd9a-eadf-11e9-9c6d-436a0df4f31d_story.html.

204. For definitive examinations of world order definitions and practices, see Kissinger, *A World Restored*; Kissinger, *Diplomacy*; and Kissinger, *World Order* (New York: Penguin Press, 2014).

205. There is some controversy regarding whether da Vinci actually said this. A version of this quote has also been attributed to Johann Wolfgang von Goethe, *The Maxims and Reflections of Goethe*, trans. Bailey Saunders (London: Macmillan, 1906), 130.

ABOUT THE AUTHOR

Robert D. Blackwill is the Henry A. Kissinger senior fellow for U.S. foreign policy at the Council on Foreign Relations. He is also the Diller-von Furstenberg Family Foundation distinguished scholar at the Henry A. Kissinger Center for Global Affairs at Johns Hopkins University's School of Advanced International Studies. He is a former deputy assistant to the president, deputy national security advisor for strategic planning, and presidential envoy to Iraq under President George W. Bush. He was U.S. ambassador to India from 2001 to 2003. In 2016 he became the first U.S. ambassador to India since John Kenneth Galbraith to receive the Padma Bhushan Award from the government of India for distinguished service of a high order. From 1989 to 1990, he was special assistant to President George H.W. Bush for European and Soviet affairs, during which he was awarded the Commander's Cross of the Order of Merit by the Federal Republic of Germany for his contribution to German unification. Earlier in his career, he was the U.S. ambassador to conventional arms negotiations with the Warsaw Pact, director for European affairs at the National Security Council, principal deputy assistant secretary of state for political-military affairs, and principal deputy assistant secretary of state for European affairs. Blackwill is the author and editor of many articles and books on transatlantic relations, Russia and the West, the greater Middle East, and Asian security. His latest book, *War by Other Means: Geoeconomics and Statecraft*, coauthored with Jennifer M. Harris, was named a best foreign policy book of 2016 by *Foreign Affairs*.

Made in the USA
San Bernardino, CA
04 May 2020